THE TERRACED MOUNTAIN

THE TERRACED MOUNTAIN

W.F. LANTRY

FIRST EDITION

Little Red Tree Publishing, LLC,

Copyright © 2015 W.F. Lantry

All rights are reserved under International and Pan-American Copyright Conventions. Except for brief passages quoted in a newspaper, magazine, radio or television review, no part of this book may be reproduced in any form or by any means, electronic or mechanical, including photocopying and recording, or by any information storage and retrieval system, without permission in writing from the publisher.

Layout and Cover Design: Michael Linnard
Text in Minion Pro, Trajan Pro and Ariel.

First Edition, 2015, manufactured in USA
1 2 3 4 5 6 7 8 9 10   LSI   20 19 18 17 16 15

All previous publication credits of the poems in this collection are listed at the back of this book on page 103.

Front cover photograph is from an article on the website: www.vietscene.net, by ngocphuongnh called "Dazzling Beauty of Mu Cang Chai," August 7, 2015. The original photos has been slightly altered to focus on the terraced mountains of Mu Cang Chai.

Author photograph, on page 105 and back cover, was taken by Avonlee Photography and is reproduced here by kind permission.

Photograph of Kathleen Fiztpatrick Lantry on the back cover singing was taken by the author.

Library of Congress Cataloging-in-Publication Data

Lantry, W.F.
  The terraced Mountain / W.F. Lantry. -- 1st ed.
     p. cm.
  Includes glossary and index.
  ISBN 978-1-935656-41-8 (pbk. : alk. paper)
  I. Title.
  PS3612.A58565S77 2015
  811'.6--dc23

Little Red Tree Publishing LLC
www.littleredtree.com

This book is dedicated to Kathleen Fitzpatrick,
with thanks and admiration.

"So may our legend last while verse endures,
And all that time my name be linked with yours."

Contents

Acknowledgements	xi
Introduction by W.F. Lantry	xv

Meditation I – The Terraced Mountain   1

In the Garden	3
Pilgrimage	4
Palisades	5
Thorns	6
The Garden of Nuts	7
Climbing	8
Bridge	9
Candlemaker	10
Shoemaker	11
The Untier of Knots	12
Glassmaker	13
Earthquakes	14
Goldsmith	15
Loom	16
Bird Song	17
Petals	18
The Fall	19
Wings	20
Emptiness	21
Candleflame	22
Marriage	23
Cantata	24
Eudaimonia	25
Self-control	26

Gentleness	27
Goodness	28
Patience	29
Kindness	30
Peace	31

Meditation II – Charismata Canticle — 33

Music Vigil	35
Intricate Forms Lead to Contemplation	36
Ubi Caritas	37
Muérome de Amores, Carillo	38
Bridge Across the River	39
Ave Maria	40
Canticle	41
This Is How a Person Becomes a Flowering Orchard	42
Robe of Beauty	43
Cien Ovejas	44
Mariposa	45
Shekhinah	46
Panis Angelicus	47
Aqua de Vida	48
Another Kind of Beauty	49
The One Breath	50
Fountain	51
Lorica of St. Patrick	52
Epithalamium	53
The Inner Light of Blossoms	54
Via Pulchritudinis	55
Claritatis	56
Rhapsody	57
Coloratura	58
Charismata	59
Be the Mirror of Life in the Eyes of the Dove	60
Viriditas	61
Feather	62
Reflection	63

Meditation III – Brother Sun, Sister Moon   65

Correspondence	67
The Relinquishing	68
Calibrations	69
Recessional	70
From La Brigue	71
From Isola 2000	72
Note from Paradise	73
Great Silence	74
One Song	75
From the Baie des Anges	76
Consolation	77
At Chartres	78
A Tongue of Fire	79
The Shared Path	80
Lavender Blossoms	81
Water of Life	82
Whirlpool	83
Fisherman	84
Interior Melodies	85
Intertwined Light	86
From Three Islands	87
Dark Night	88
From the Edge	89
Last Journey	90
The Twisted Knot	91
Rustic Cross	92
Untier of Knots	93
Ripples	94
The Visit	95
Index of Titles and first lines	97
Publication Credits	103
About the Author	105

Acknowledgements

A Few Thoughts About Unearned Grace

We sit at our desks, confronted daily with the tyranny of the blank page, the blank screen. It's easy for doubt to creep into the shadows around us, for despair to fill our hearts. "What if I start to write, and nothing's there?" "What if I'm going in the wrong direction?"

I was having dinner, years ago, with a celebrated writer, who I knew worked every day. "Don't you have those same doubts?" I asked. "Yes," she said, "and no. I walk to the well every day, a little bit worried, but I've always found water in the well."

The idea of an eternal source, an ever-flowing spring, is comforting. But it's not enough, we need companions, and I've been blessed with many over the last few years, people whose kind words and gracious actions have kept me going, even when things seemed most difficult, even when I'd done nothing to merit such kindness.

One day, feeling in disgrace with fortune and men's eyes, all alone beweeping my outcast fate, I received a message from an editor, Beth Bates, who was sending me galleys of some stories she was about to publish in her journal. As a side note, while discussing technical details, she wrote "I envy you your writing life." I was completely taken aback, since I'd been focusing, as we all do, on the difficulties. She helped me realize we should celebrate even the smallest things, to "clap our hands and sing, and louder sing!" Thank you, Beth.

I do some moderation work on a poetry site, contributing to the poetics discussions as well as I can. It's not always the most peaceful place, and I get a little frustrated sometimes. One day, I was sitting at a picnic table during a break at a writer's conference, and a shy young poet, Nausheen Eusuf, sat down next to me to talk. I mentioned my frustration, and thoughts of quitting. And she said, "Please don't quit. I never say anything there, but I read everything you write, and I know many others who do the same. Keep going, if only for our sakes." I hope I can be as kind and generous as she is someday.

Early on in our project, Kate Bernadette Benedict accepted a few poems. Later we worked together on her journal. She calls herself "the other Kate," to distinguish herself from my wife. Her early belief in my work was critical in an uncertain time.

And there are many other editors whose support has been gratifying: Richard Peabody, Edward Byrne, Dan Veach. Ann Drysdale wrote all the way from England asking for a poem included in this book, Amy Burns wrote from Scotland. Kathleen Kirk, a fine poet in her own name, requested some for a lovely journal she edits, pairing writers and artists. Helene Cardona, jet-setting between, I presume, Malibu and Paris, chose some for Levure Littéraire. Chris Lott requested stories and poems for the very first issue of Eclectica. Editors are good people, who do things out of love, and I love working with Linda Simoni-Wastila, and Firestone Feinberg.

We live in an electronic world now, and exceptional people are doing unimagined things at the intersection of art and technology. Mary Ann Sullivan is one of these, doing beautifully spiritual work at *Tower Journal*. We've done some nice collaborations with Nic Sebastian, of "Very Like a Whale" fame. Alexandra Oliver at *The Rotary Dial*, Don Zirilli at *Now Culture*, Charles Musser at *Soundzine*, Marie Fitzpatrick at *The Linnet's Wings*, these are all people making art relevant in the digital age. I'm proud to know them, even if we've never met in person.

Sometimes it gets difficult when the physical and digital worlds collide. Gregory Dowling risked reputation and career to allow me to participate in a special workshop. And yet, I sat right next to him at a pizza parlor in New York City, and didn't recognize him.

Although we'd talked online for years, he actually had to introduce himself. I can be very dense sometimes! At other times, things go better: I finally met Yibing Huang, a poet and editor from China, at a reading near Harvard Square, and discovered we had a personal connection as strong as any begun in the physical world. I think the same would happen if I ever met Michelle Elvy, but right now she's on a sailboat, traversing the Indian Ocean with her family, and our only connection is through her laptop. I envy her wandering life.

On my screen, I get messages from old friends who I haven't seen in years, Avril Vnct (yes, that's the name she uses online,) her husband Bruno, both in Paris, Neil Clarke in Madrid, Kathryn Bender somewhere in the Carolinas, Craig Parker somewhere out west in Portlandia. None of them are writers, but their messages cheer me, they know how to make me feel as if someone's in my corner. I can't find adequate words to say how helpful that is.

I was asked to participate in a research project at Hopkins a couple years back, and through that project I met Bill Richards, who taught me the virtues and practice of contemplation and meditation. Few people have had such an effect of my day to day life. During that time, I met Sandy Travis Bildahl, an artist based in Annapolis. We all went through some very intense spiritual experiences together, and Sandy doesn't know it, but she and Mary Cosimano helped to keep me grounded.

There are a few people who deserve affectionate mention. Joani Reese and I talk more about home repair and improvement than we do about poetry and fiction, but that's how we first met. Susan Tepper has been extraordinarily kind to Kate and I, arranging readings, arranging publications, always always being supportive. Annabelle Moseley published us in her journal and invited us to read at the Long Island Violin Shop—the dignity and respect with which she treats her poetic colleagues is all too rare in our present informal world. Quincy Lehr set up several readings in New York, and even solicited poetic essays. I think of him as a modern day comrade at arms.

But I've saved the most special mention for just a few. First among these is Tammy Ho Lai-Ming, poet and editor from Hong Kong, with whom Kate and I have developed a special bond. When I first met Yvette Neisser Moreno, I could tell she was the real thing, a true poet in every sense of the word, with all that implies. She only lives a few miles away, as does Ed Shacklee, who I think of as a kind of brother. And my actual brother, James Lantry, namesake to my youngest son. I know he doesn't always understand what I'm talking about, but he's always on my side. As is Ro Mauro Clarke, who helps celebrate even the smallest good news that comes to Kate and me, and even buys the surplus eggs from our backyard chickens.

A few months after Kate and I started this project, we met Maryann Corbett. She was largely unknown at the time, but we've watched her success and reputation grow. She's now covered in prizes and laurel crowns, books and essays seem to flow out of her easily, her name is on the wind everywhere. No-one deserves it more, and we deeply value her support and friendship.

Finally, there's Michael Linnard. The relationship between writer and publisher is something to be cherished, there's no other like it. And it must be symbiotic: Michael, who does such beautiful design with all the books he publishes, is simply hopeless when it comes to the digital world. So I have the honor of configuring and curating his website, programming for his special needs, translating his vision into electronic code. I like to think we're good for each other, and I strongly believe we are.

Thanks to everyone I've mentioned, and especially thanks to all those for whom there simply isn't room to mention. Hundreds, thousands of writing friends, all over the world, each one playing a special role. I'm never alone at the keyboard, they're all with me, present at every moment, urging me on. My work is theirs. Whenever my mind turns to them, I recall those words of Yeats:

> "Think where man's glory most begins and ends,
> and say my glory was: I had such friends!"

Introduction

I

On my birthday, not so many years ago, my wife came to me and sat me down for a serious talk.

"What are you doing?" she said. "You're wasting your life. You're a writer, and you haven't written anything in years. I know you're doing important work, but it's not what you were put here to do. So I'll make you this deal. I know you don't like sending things out for publication. But you can write. So if you write something, every day, I'll send it out. Your role, from now on, is just to write."

"OK," I said, "but what should I write?"

"You let me worry about that. I'll do the research. I'll correspond with the editors. We'll do this together."

And so began one of the most prolific collaborations in recent memory. True to her word, she did the research, she found the journals, the calls for submissions. I'd be at my desk at work, late in the day, and I'd receive a message saying, "I need a poem, under 30 lines, about rivers or shorelines. Don't bother coming home for dinner until it's done." Or "I need a story, under a thousand words, with a scene in a restaurant. And be quick about it, the deadline is midnight and I have to go to rehearsal tonight, so you'll have to watch the boys."

Every day.

We started in March, the end of March. I wrote and wrote. Even though she knew nothing about the literary world (she's a Coloratura soprano), she started writing editors. The acceptances began to come in. Journals, especially quarterlies, have similar schedules. June 1st is a big day for them. And it was for us: nine poems came out that day, in four different journals. My first publications in years. Strike that. Our first publications.

She started planning excursions: museums, trips to the ocean, cultural events in town. Every trip had a purpose: another story, food for thought, another poem. And she was nearly miraculous. One Tuesday evening, in spite of my grumbling, she dragged me to go hear a former poet laureate read at the Folger Theater. I scratched a poem on the back of the program as we listened. When I was done, she grabbed the paper. The poem was published by a web journal based in Indonesia on Saturday.

All over the country, all over the world, poems and stories were getting accepted and published. I think she's up to thirty countries at this point. We started to win literary prizes. It was, she was, astonishing. I learned to listen carefully. I learned to do exactly what she asked.

Late September. We were side by side on the bed after a long day, and she was searching the web for new worlds to explore. "William," she said, "have you ever written a mystical poem?"

I knew about mystical poetry, at least a little: St. John of the Cross, Teresa of Avila, Mirabai, Attar. But I was more of a love poet, or poems about craft, about making things. I'm a woodworker, and not exactly the most churchgoing person who ever lived. So I was a little puzzled by her question. "Why do you ask?"

"Well, there's this thing I just found today: Premio Mundial Fernando Rielo de Poesía Mística." "My Spanish isn't good, can you translate?" "The Rielo Worldwide Prize in Mystical Poetry. There's a deadline coming up."

I had no idea what she was asking, but like I said, I've learned to listen. And I'd read Leo Durocher's biography, where as a young prospect, the manager asks him, "Hey kid, have you ever played shortstop?" And the kid replies, "Sure. Lots of times."

"When's the deadline?" I asked. "It has to be in Madrid by October 15th." "No problem," I said, turning away to think about something else. She stopped me. "There's only one tiny little difficulty. It has to be at least six hundred lines long."

Like I said, I'm a lyric poet, and like any lyric poet, I can dash off a sonnet in fifteen minutes. But six hundred lines? In an unfamiliar genre? In less than two weeks? Why had I spoken so carelessly?

There's one thing you need to know about Kate. She's very devout, maybe the most devout Catholic I've ever known. She goes to daily Mass, she's a music director at the largest parish around, it's not unusual for her to sing in four or five different churches on a weekend. I could see in her eyes this meant something to her. Surely, after all she'd done, I could do something for her.

And so it started. I spent the first day drafting a plan for writing. Mystical poems are strange things, filled with numbers and symbols, allusions and layers. Every line in Dante has four different meanings. As a man drowning grasps a floating log, just to keep his head above water, I grasped a theme: Our Lady of Guadalupe. I wanted to write poems like prayers, like the beads of a rosary. But a rosary is too long. Kate told me about Chaplets, small things, like rosaries, but with fewer beds.

Kate made me a chaplet.

The intermediate beads are green, and three larger clear beads separate them. At the end, there's another clear bead, and she attached a medal for Our Lady. The beads are arranged in the plan of the poem: four short sections, a longer one, four short sections, all the way around. I kept it wrapped around my hand while writing, I started carrying it around with me all the time. To remember.

And I wrote. I got up early and wrote in the morning. I stayed up late, and wrote in my office at home. As I wrote, I knew Kate was praying feverishly just on the other side of the wall. It kept me going. The chaplet kept me going. And something else kept me going, something I can't explain. I was filled with joy and sadness at once. Real joy. Joy so profound I'd sit at my desk weeping as I wrote. I felt a presence around me, like a living light, which lit up everything inside me, as long as I kept writing. And when I was done, each time, it would fade. The feeling drove me on. I was happy to sit down to write the next section. They built on each other, one by one. And finally, the poem was done.

I should have felt a sense of elation, of accomplishment. But all I felt was sadness. The light was fading. Would it ever return? How could I get it back? But there was no time to think of that. We had one day to proof read, to fix any errors, to smooth out any rough edges. Kate added the punctuation and formatting. I read it one last time. And she sent it off to Madrid.

To be honest, I pretty much forgot about it: there were other projects, other deadlines to meet, a busy family to care for. Life goes on.

Six weeks later, I was in a meeting at work, and my phone started ringing. I ignored it. It rang again, and I turned it down. But it just kept buzzing and buzzing. Finally, I excused myself, and took the call.

"William," she whispered, "William, your poem is a finalist. Three hundred books of poems, from thirty countries, and you're one of twelve finalists. We might have to fly to Rome. We need passports, new clothes for you. I need a new dress." I closed my eyes, and thought about it. And we waited.

But the call from Rome never came. Kate was disappointed. "Next year," she said. "Next year?" I said. "Are you kidding me?"

But of course next year came around, and I had to do as she asked. It's now been seven years, and we've been finalists four times. No-one writing in English has ever won. Spanish is the first language of everyone on the jury. But I keep going, mostly to honor her. And because the light returns whenever I write.

II

Three of the poems are collected here. "The Terraced Mountain" tells the story of a spiritual marriage, in the form of a journey. You won't notice as you're reading, but it really is about my life with Kate. She points the way, providing direction, and I supply the energy and strength. When the wall between each terrace is too high for her to climb, I push her up, or climb it first and pull her up.

Another thing you may overlook: I had in mind Dante's spiritual mountain, with its various representative levels. The two pilgrims together move from one level to the next, overcoming, learning as they go. It may help to think of Thomas Merton's *Seven Story Mountain*, as well. But neither Dante nor Merton spoke of this particular peak.

The two travelers begin in a garden, where there's a kind of fruitful bliss. Everything seems harmonious. But of course a storm arrives. There are storms in every marriage, no matter how peaceful. They need to move on, and start walking together. She sees a better place, and as they move towards higher ground, she starts to sing.

It's not as easy as all that. The mountain is surrounded by a wall they must climb over. And on the other side, there are many thorned bushes they have to make their way through. It is not done with ease. At last they reach the lowest slopes, where there's an orchard growing, and a quiet pool. A place where they can rest and contemplate. It's a walnut orchard, and they can examine the mirrored halves of the fruit, the intricacies held inside.

The pool is made by a stream, and they follow the stream up the hillside. They find a wall, with shards of broken pottery around the base. They find a passageway to the next level, and then a bridge across the stream.

They begin meeting people on the terraces: a candlemaker, a glassworker, a cobbler. Each stitch the shoemaker sews is woven with his faith. A woman sits in a small room, untying knots.

Have you ever been high up in the mountains? Really high up, above the timberline? I remember being in the Sierra Nevadas, and realizing the mountains, which looked so solid, were actually constantly shaken by tiny earthquakes. At night, when everything was quiet, I could hear the stones rolling down their slopes. And so with this mountain: each seemingly unshakeable terrace is ringed with broken stone, and they need to clamber over the scree to reach the next level.

They find a goldsmith there, and a weaver of tapestries. All along the way, they can hear the songs of unseen birds, high above them. Small flowers grow in the rockface, on the terrace walls, everywhere there's a tiny, delicate beauty. But as they climb up, she slips.

Somehow, she doesn't fall. It's almost as if a hand, not my own, reached down and caught her. I've never felt that way. My own experience of faith is more like quiet contemplation. But she feels renewed by the incident. They rest together in a small house on the next terrace, watching a candle blaze in the quiet dark. And in that small house, their marriage is renewed.

The next day, she walks along, singing in the daylight. This is what happiness is: walking together over the earth towards a goal. Together, they share the Fruit of the Spirit: Gentleness,

Goodness, Patience, Self-control, Kindness, Peace. These are the things a marriage is built on. And they drink together from the source of the stream.

III

"Charismata Canticle": what a title! A charism is a gift, a canticle is a song, so this is my tribute to Kate's gift of song. People throw words like that around, but in her case, it's really true. And it's a gift she shares with thousands of people every week, at Weddings and Funerals and Masses.

What great joy she brings to the people who hear her! Even at Funerals: I have seen her stand up, in front of many weeping people, and start to sing. I've watched the beauty of her voice calm their grief, change their countenance. I've heard her song give comfort even in the most difficult of times, add to the celebratory joy of Weddings, and give the worshipers reason to believe they can accede to perpetual beauty. Her voice draws back the veil hanging between our quotidian world and the Eternal.

She sings for the living, she even sings for those near death. That's really the origin of this poem: she was called to the room of a dying man, and asked to sing "Ave Maria" as he passed. It was transformative for everyone there.

I was walking in the forest that morning, and knew nothing about it. Instead, I was thinking about the complexity of the leaves, how their patterns seemed to match the forms of the streams I crossed. And so the poem is built, back and forth, between song and forest.

Rilke wondered when we're truly alive. Kate is most alive when she's singing. Where that delicate beauty comes from, I can't say, but whenever I hear her I'm filled with gratitude, the way John of the Cross was filled with gratitude when he heard singing outside his monk's cell.

Perhaps it's the same gratitude I find in nature, perhaps her voice is like a bridge from one shore to another, a way to connect the two, and restore the harmony broken by separation. It's hard to say. I only know those who listen feel a kind of ecstasy. And in that ecstasy each of us may find our lives flourishing.

Yeats said, "I made my song a coat, out of old embroideries," but her song is more like a robe of flame, lighting the world around her with a sweet eternal light, illuminating things we never notice otherwise. Still, those things are always there, like the small wings of dragonflies in sunlight just above the stream's surface. Perhaps her voice allows us to look more closely, to see the beauty all around us.

Why are we here? To add to the world, to reinvent beauty, to co-create the earth? That was Hildegard's answer nine hundred years ago, and it still feels like a good answer. The leaves fall one by one, we ourselves fall like the leaves, and yet that beauty remains. The water of life continues to flow. The boundaries of experience dissolve in contemplation of the beautiful, and the miracle of grace flows into us.

I make things out of wood and metal and words. I can touch them, I can write them down and preserve them. But the beauty she creates is both timeless and only in the moment, carried on the very air we breathe.

I'm a gardener, a builder of ponds for growing lotus and waterlilies, and so water and fountains hold a special place in my life. But sometimes I think of water as something else entirely, something flowing through all of us.

I've also studied the history of songs and hymns. How we sometimes sing to keep up our courage, whistle past graveyards. And yet, her song isn't like that at all. It frees us from all fear and uncertainty, and lets us walk in peace.

Take her Wedding songs, how she sings as the bride lays flowers at Mary's feet, and shows us the harmony at the beginning of the couple's journey. Her voice allows the possibility of blissful consolation in the shared community of the ceremony.

You won't believe me, but if you go out into the garden at dusk, after sunset, and look very closely, the flowers seem to have their own inner light, almost as if the light came from within themselves. Her songs have the same feel: they seem to come from within her, even if we know their origin is elsewhere.

There are many paths to Paradise. But the path of beauty seems the best: the way light moves through stained glass, the colored clarity a metaphor for spiritual energy, burning through the air as a living flame. Perhaps that same energy drives the growth of both forest and stream, and moves us along our journey.

I mention stained glass because of the name of her gift: she's a Coloratura. Yes, that's a term of art, and it means her voice can color sound, add jewel tones to harmonies. It's such a profound experience, people carry it with them throughout the day, and its recollection illuminates their lives, reinvents the earth.

'Mystical' simply means direct experience of the divine. But it's not as if we need to hear a voice from above, or see letters written in fire across the sky. It's more about opening ourselves and allowing something to flow into us. Something that may fill us with inexplicable peace.

One time I was sitting in Mass, listening to her sing. And I noticed a dove had accidentally flown into the church. I watched a bit of down, a small feather, floating on the air for as long as her song lasted. It was so light, it simply drifted among the rafters, never settling. At least not while she was still singing.

How many times have I seen light coming through windows as I listened to her sing? She says her goal is to help us pray, she says whoever sings well prays twice. But I think there's something more than that: the light is like flame, and it burns within us whenever we hear her.

IV

My middle name is Francis, so naturally the prayers of St. Francis are special to me. The real ones, the ones he actually spoke. Like his prayer to creation, reflected in the title of the final poem of this collection: "Brother Sun, Sister Moon."

This is a poem of journey and of loss. It's written to my eldest brother, who died not long ago, but shaped much of my youth. And to a teacher who also shaped my youth, and is now a cloistered nun. Since I can't visit either of them, it's written in the form of letters, the letters I should have sent them as I moved through my life's journey, the letters I never wrote.

What can we carry with us? When I began backpacking, I quickly learned we always take too much, far more than we need. Better to leave all that stuff behind, and walk with lighter steps.

My father taught me all the steps for rebuilding cars. Patience and care are required. I learned how not to get ahead of myself, how to measure tolerances as exactly as possible, and how every task seems to require a little blood before it's done.

My first flight in an airplane was halfway around the world. I looked down as I flew over the Arctic, that vast expanse of ice and water, then landed in London and took the train all the way down to Provence.

There's an old chapel there, way up in the Alps, built in Medieval times. The frescoes are horrifying: monsters consume the sinners, while everything is flame around them. They were created after Dante and Aquinas: it's hard to imagine people once associated such things with the beatific vision.

I learned to ski in the Alps. But we carry our memories with us, and the grains of snow blowing across the surface reminded me of the grains of sand blowing across the deserts of my youth.

One of the beautiful things about the Mediterranean region is you can leave the snow covered mountains in the morning, and find yourself among flourishing vineyards by afternoon. I found such a place, a small farmhouse as old as any chapel, orchards and fields and ponds brimming with trout. 'Who quarrels over half-pennies, that plucks the trees for bread?'

Of course, I was writing then. It's solitary work done in near silence, and often filled with doubt. What a relief to walk down to the beach at evening, and see something as simple and immediate as sardine fishermen spreading their nets in preparation for tomorrow's fish market!

The hills along the coastline are covered with terraces, where olives, cherries and vines grow. I walked paths dating from Roman times, hearing the same sounds the ancient gardeners heard: the fox's cry, the distant barking of wild dogs.

Sometimes I went down to visit the port and watched women mending the nets that had been spread in the sunlight to dry. Near the Bay of Angels, the untier of knots had to have the same patience I'd learned on what was now a distant shore.

And yet, it still felt foreign to me, even after living there many years. There were unexplained sounds in the night, unnameable creatures moving about. I kept the lamplight burning, even as I fell asleep.

I love cathedrals, the huge arched ceilings designed and crafted by human hands to give us a glimpse of the eternal, the marble columns like tree trunks rising into the air, the tiled labyrinths hidden within the floor.

But elaborate as those cathedrals are, my own life was simple, barely furnished. A table and chair and bed were enough for my purposes, a lamp or candle to light my work. And always, just at the edge of my vision, the unfamiliar shadows flickering.

Sometimes I walked the mountains, since they reminded me of where I'd walked in earlier years, and sometimes I lingered there too long before turning back. Lost in the growing darkness, in a foreign place, I could almost mistake them for home.

And even though the birds there were different, their flights seemed the same, and the flowers reminded me of my early gardens. I gave myself over to unplanned steps, followed wherever the pathways happened to lead. We only discover new things when we become completely lost. Deep, quiet, secret things, unknown but familiar. How can we remember them? How can we know which way to turn? But if we follow our spirit's path, we may arrive at peaceful, unexpected places: a mountain pool, unmarked on any map.

Or we can follow the stream feeding the pool, bend down along the bank, and drop a fishing line into the water. We can find a kind of joy in the waiting, practice patience while we watch the evening birds, knowing we can always find our way back to camp, even in moonlight.

For the moonlight shines on the broken granite, on the veins of quartz flowing through the rocks. And the constellations turn above our heads, harmonious, and seem to reverberate within us, until we become one with the landscape, or until the landscape repeats us.

We are like those slopes, those leaves falling, like the blue flax blooming between the stones, in the colors of Mary. Shouldn't we be singing, even when we're lost, shouldn't we be walking the unfamiliar earth with a sense of joy?

There are lakes to discover, and islands within the lakes, with willows and cottonwoods and sycamores, those lovers of water. No gardener would place them there, and yet their unexpected beauty fills out hearts.

But even among such beauty, we can lose our way. If the moon goes behind clouds, we can find ourselves completely lost. The dark night of the soul is real, and we feel ourselves bereft, abandoned, with nowhere to turn, the cliffs falling away on all sides, and no way back.

It's best to stop then, and wait for light. But as the sun rises, the white granite, scintillating all around, reflects the light like a snowbank, and we can lose our sight. I still can't say what happened: something led me back up the slope, over the broken stones, guiding me forward, as long as I kept moving.

My brother had a similar journey. His ended differently. But I know, without knowing, every step he took, since I walked them myself. I know the despair of the silence he felt when there was no voice to guide him.

How can we voice such despair, such loss, especially when we feel it within ourselves? Our very hearts are knotted, like those torn nets along the shore. Who could ever untangle them?

Too late, I visited his place of rest among the junipers of the desert mountains. The red dust blew over our eyes, a small cross marked an insignificant spot. There was nothing to do but pray: "now, and at the hour of our death..."

Yet Francis praised the day, praised the sun and moon, both the dawn and the dusk. I remember swallowtail butterflies, their wings dancing in unplanned movements. I remember the way the light felt on my skin, the way the breeze swirled around us.

Now I live in a forest, on the other side of the continent. The flashing wings still look foreign to me. The river behind our house changes constantly. I know I should walk in sadness, but I'm filled with joy, as if my brother could see all the miracles of the earth through my eyes, as if his voice were mine.

What epilogue could we have, after so many years? We visited the monastery, only for a little while. Then Sister too was gone: we sat in the church, all the sisters hidden from sight, as they sang songs of joy and grace.

W.F. Lantry,
Washington, D.C. 2015

MEDITATION I

THE TERRACED MOUNTAIN

Flowers appear on the earth;
the season of singing has come,
the cooing of doves
is heard in our land.
The fig tree forms its early fruit;
the blossoming vines spread their fragrance.
Arise, come, my darling;
my beautiful one, come with me.

~ Song of Songs 2:12-13

In the Garden

A rose with thirteen petals greets the air
each morning, lights our pathway and perfumes
this land: our garden, fields, orchards, vines,
the tender earth we gently cultivate
together: she, exact, traces the lines
for me to dig. Our work among these blooms
bears patient fruit, and leaves some room for grace

to weave through intersections of this place.
A balanced harmony, a living flame
of love persists and grows into a blaze
until our careful actions replicate
the symmetry around us, and the rays
of sun construct a lattice: each the same,
warming our work, lighting our artistry

with endlessly renewing energy
until, one day, stormclouds begin to build
far in the East, then spread, and start to rain,
unbalanced, uncontained: floods inundate
our orchard, vineyard- what had been a plain
becomes a rushing stream that can't be stilled
and we must leave, sharing a quiet prayer.

Pilgrimage

"Where can we go?" I asked, looking around
at those wide waters swirling past the rows
we'd planted carefully. She said, "I've seen
on cloudless days a mountain in the West
rising against the sky. I felt serene
each time I saw it." Gathering our clothes
and little else, we started out. No road

revealed itself to us. Our progress slowed
each time the waters deepened, but we made
our way as best we could. I watched her eyes
and found direction there. As we progressed
the waters grew more shallow, and the skies
stopped raining. Looking eastward, I surveyed
the place we'd left. Our home, and everything

we'd built was gone. Yet she began to sing!
whether from habit, or from joy. Her voice
gave me new strength. I turned and followed on
for I could see the mountain now, its crest
terraced against the sky, its outline drawn
as if by hand. I started to rejoice
as we moved quickly towards more solid ground.

Palisades

We find the mountain's base, and find a wall
blocking our path: a ring of well-laid stone
too high to climb. We walk along its length
searching for breaches, fallen blocks, or gates,
but finding none. I do not have the strength
even to break the mortar, which has grown
solid from years of weathering. We find

a quarry nearby. All this stone was mined
outside the wall! And so, the unseen hands
who built it, worked from this side, to prevent
themselves from climbing, lifted those great weights
and placed them here to block their own ascent!
We hear something, and turn: a songbird stands
atop the wall, singing, and there's a vine

growing nearby. She takes it as a sign
and says, "We must climb here." But there's no hold.
I lift her to my shoulders, and she grasps
the vine, and clambers to the top. She waits
then turns, and reaches down, until she clasps
my hand, and in a scramble, uncontrolled
I make the top, lose balance, turn, and fall.

Thorns

I fell among the briars, brambles, spines.
Thorns ripped my skin, and crying out, I bled,
but raised myself, and stood. I helped her down.
We stood there, lost: no path along the wall,
all progress blocked, bent canes tearing her gown,
twisting their arches well above my head.
I turned to her. She said, "Let's move away

from this stone wall. See how the branches sway
in chaos, and see how the shadows match
their patterns on this ground, then disappear?
Follow those shadows." So I pushed the tall
first canes aside. They parted. I could clear
enough room for my limbs, and let her catch
each branch before it whipped back into place

as we moved forward through that thorn-filled
space.
The field was mostly mud, and yet the ground
was filled with roots: enough to hold our weight.
When losing strength, I thought I heard the call
of perching birds, and bent our pathway straight
towards the cadence of their guiding sound,
and we passed through the interlacing vines.

The Garden of Nuts

We had not asked for water or for shade
and yet we found an orchard with a stream
running between the trunks of ancient trees.
She paused a moment where the waters made
a quiet pool. Sinking to her knees,
she drank with gratitude. The surface gleam
mirrored sunlight, and lit the underside

of long, paired leaves, uniting the divide
of light and shadow. All around us, round,
thick husks of nuts had fallen, sometimes green
and some dried brown: in sunlight, they would fade
and crack. I picked one up. Held in between
my hands, I noticed two smooth halves surround
the patterned shell. They dyed my fingers black

as I looked closely. Then pulling them back,
I reached the shell. I summoned all my strength
and opened it, finding the mirrored parts
within: two halves now perfectly arrayed,
repeating, back and forth, as if two hearts
pulsed in a single form along its length,
like layered patterns on her gown's brocade.

Climbing

We rested in the orchard for a time,
then followed the descending watercourse
upstream, until we found the sloping base
of the first terrace. Broken shards of pots
littered the ground, an almost perfect vase
with an unglazed lip, displayed its coarse
clay underlay. How had it fallen here?

Its sides described a nearly perfect sphere
but something had gone wrong. We turned away
and started climbing up the random blocks,
my hand, above, held hers: in certain spots
the stones detached and wobbled. Tiny rocks
broke loose and fell in raucous disarray.
We marked their falling, turned, and climbed again,

and felt the slope, once vertical, begin
to ease a bit. Her hand left mine. She leapt
from block to block so lightly, almost danced
upwards in pirouette—as if the thought
of reaching terraced ground gave lightness—glanced
a moment back, and then, cautious, she stepped
to the first level, finishing her climb.

Bridge

I followed her. We found ourselves in light
on a wide terrace ringing the tall peak.
It stretched and curved away around the ridge.
Small buildings marked the landscape. Where the wide
stream crossed the plain, someone had built a bridge
of stone and rough-hewn wood, carved with unique
and unfamiliar images, like wings

spread full in flight, or twigs a closed beak brings
to weave into a nest so intricate
its very form confounds an untrained eye,
as wood and air and bark all coincide,
weaving straight lines until their curves defy
our insight, and their woven patterns knit
themselves into a form we understand

only after we let our hearts expand.
This place seemed new to us, we dared not turn,
move forward or move back, and so we stood
until a woman beckoned us inside
her small workshop, rough-framed in willow wood,
to darkness where a single flame might burn
and light the earth, renewing our lost sight.

Candlemaker

The workshop crafted candles, elements
of fabrication scattered everywhere
were brought together by that woman's hands.
She started with a single cotton braid
first doubled, then redoubled, until strands
were lost within the weavings, and the spare
beauty of simple lines grew rich with knots.

She cut the wicks to length, hooked them in slots
of wooden handles, dipped them into warmed
vessels of wax, and hung them from a line.
She murmured as she worked. Her voice conveyed,
as if patience were part of the design,
a calm concern for how the candles formed.
She straightened each, then dipped them back within

those vessels until layers built again,
over and over. Halfway through, she etched
a small image on each. It disappeared
with the next layer, and was overlaid
a dozen times. Then finishing, she peered
as closely as a watchmaker, and stretched
the candles straight on crafted implements.

Shoemaker

We came across a woman sitting outside
in deep sunlight, with coiled ropes nearby,
each knotted hopelessly. She would take one,
examine it, and hold it up to light,
knowing somewhere she'd see a hint of sun,
and that small hint might help her hands untie
or loosen, just a bit, the tangled strain.

She worked a little, held it up again,
and worked a little more. But each one held
a twisted knot too dense for human hands
to unplait: too contorted, pulled too tight.
For these she used a metal spike: the bands
would give way. Her dexterity compelled
their opening, and searching, she would find

a pathway that might lead her to unbind,
with gentle artistry, each hidden knot.
Once done she stretched each rope to its whole length
then, splicing carefully, she'd reunite
each to the longer whole, restore the strength
it held within itself when it was wrought
before misworking let it become tied.

The Untier of Knots

The next shop housed a shoemaker, whose task
seemed endless: broken shoes were everywhere:
torn soles, split heels, each shattered record told
of wanderings across a broken land
and of the struggles pilgrimages hold
even in peaceful times. A humble chair
and bench, his only furniture, long braids

of leather hung nearby in rough cascades.
He worked in silence, noticed us, and said,
"Each stitch I weave, I weave for God, and each
renews our earth. Our humble acts expand
across each level, amplify, and reach
even unquiet hearts." We watched him thread
laces through simple holes, we watched him bind

fragments together, until, intertwined
by subtle craft, what had been two became
a single, nearly seamless entity.
Watching him work, we came to understand
how simple acts renew identity,
reveal unseen patterns, and reframe
those questions we had hardly known to ask.

Glassmaker

A man stood at a crucible. It glowed
with inner light, and on the workshop's wall
shadows mirrored his steps. A molten red
clumped on his reed. He swirled it around,
then swung the cooling mixture overhead,
blew on the reed with care, until a small
encompassed sphere took shape just at the end,

then clipped it off before it could distend.
With practiced certainty, his sharp blade etched
smooth patterns in the cooling, curving sides.
Some figures arched and stopped, while others wound
around entire forms. He used no guides,
nothing constrained his movement as he sketched
a spiral from his mind onto the sphere,

and as it cooled, the red crystal grew clear.
He picked it up, and held it in a beam
of windowed light, not looking at the source
but at the prisms suddenly unbound,
as if the light flowed through a watercourse
and leapt up suddenly out of the stream
then fell back to the vessel as it slowed.

Earthquakes

Our way was blocked by heaps of fallen stone.
We felt minute earthquakes shaking the rings
but hadn't noticed how the terraces
were broken constantly, or how the long
steep inclined walls bore renewed surfaces
of fresh stonework. Each chisel-cleft form brings
new strength, and yet, the earth's continuous

motion transforms straight lines to sinuous
tracings, as if impermanence is all,
and we two, climbing, must remake our lives,
assuming with each step the frail turn strong
and strength is weakness: anyone who strives
in certainty might tumble down this wall
or become lost, sunblinded by the split

faces of granite. Yet we must submit
ourselves to this ascending path, and bear
whatever it may hold: if we would rise
to the next broken terrace, walk along
a level trail somewhere, improvise
a passage worthy of her murmured prayer,
we must advance, calmly, through the unknown.

Goldsmith

Smoke curled from a chimnied tile roof:
the goldsmith's workshop furnace never cools.
He melts small ingots in his crucible
until the liquid surface, mirroring
his motions, makes the world visible.
He chooses carefully among his tools,
skimming dark slag away. This work refines

his mined materials, and recombines
vision and matter. Satisfied, he pours
liquid into new forms: the moistened sand
can be molded to transcribe anything-
symbol or ornament- at his command,
and as it cools, each object restores
the symmetry he's felt in silent prayer,

rebuilds a realm fallen to disrepair.
It's not enough: he breaks open the mold
revealing, underneath the rising steam,
a well cast shape, a still imperfect ring
which he must sand until it starts to gleam,
and he's reflected in the curving gold
beyond the need for complicated proof.

Loom

On wooden frames, the thread, stretched harp-string taut,
already dyed, awaits the shuttle's pass.
From nothing, from the strands of retted reeds,
the weaver fabricates a filament,
then winds it on a distaff. All she needs
is time and peace: perhaps an hourglass
to mark her progress as she moves the weft

across the warp. Working from right to left,
then back again, she tightens as she moves,
picking and battening. Her motion flows
as tides flow in and out, with elegant
precision, or as wind-blown leaves expose
the hidden patterns of this earth, the grooves
that channel every breath, mark our pathways

and guide us through the chaos of our days.
Is there a hand that guides the shuttle, or
do we, in journeying, deepen the trace
marked out by others? Do we reinvent
through work and prayer her harmonies, embrace
with motions of our own her art, restore
the patterns shuttle passages have wrought?

Bird Song

Walking along the path, we looked for ways
to climb to the next terrace, some small place
where rocks had tumbled down, forming a stair
we might ascend. Out of the cloudless sky
we heard birdsong above us in the air
and turned our gazes upwards, tried to trace
its source, but saw no wings: azure concealed

sources of melodies our ears revealed.
And yet, they must be there, warblers or wrens,
soaring too high for us to recognize,
to hold within our vision as they fly
singing on currents, as they improvise
a song to bind two realms together, cleanse
the earth and us: inflections intertwine

our hearts with beauty. Are their songs divine,
or are they sweet translations we can hear
who could not touch, in other ways, the source
awaiting us? Perhaps their songs supply
a metaphor to guide us, reinforce
our intuitions of something more clear
than eyes can comprehend in this bright haze.

Petals

We found a small plant growing in the rift
of a split stone. There seemed so little space
for anything to hold: how could those roots
find passages to reach the fertile clay?
We could not trace their paths. And yet, long shoots
lifted themselves above the cracked rockface,
encouraged by warmth and sunlight. Where they curled

tendrils into the air, ringlets unfurled,
revealing in their motions delicate
red buds, whose calyxes, in sequence, fell
onto the flashing stone. The tendrils' sway
seems almost like a dance: the small buds swell,
their changing hues describing intricate
transfigurations: metamorphosis

of green into a prism's synthesis
of every kind of light, collecting here,
almost for us, all colors into one,
as if those blossoms' beauty could convey
something eternal, even as they spun
their petals open, welcoming the clear
pure sunlight, as one welcomes a great gift.

The Fall

I wanted us to pause when light declined
and evening fell around us. But the moon,
lighting our narrow way, beckoned her on.
I followed close behind, as shadows flowed
over the rocks, as if a hand had drawn
a charcoal landscape, or someone had strewn
uncertain images across our path:

reminders of some earthquake's aftermath.
She let me move ahead, I turned, and stretched
my arm back down, and pulled her up the ledge.
We rested there a moment. Light bestowed
a softened beauty to the rough cliff edge,
where every boulder, every stone, seemed etched
eternally against the darkened sky,

when suddenly I heard a panicked cry:
she'd slipped, and I could feel the rocks cascade
pulling her down, beyond my reach. I heard
her voice, descending, come to rest, followed
by murmured thanks. She stood then, undeterred
and with new resolution, she surveyed
the path ahead, her purpose redefined.

Wings

"I can't explain. I felt dark wings surround
my spirit and they did not wish me well.
I tried to turn away," she said. "I tried
to shake them off, and yet their sound increased,
driving me back. They wanted to divide
something in me from me. That's when I fell
and cried out. Suddenly I felt a hand

holding me up. I heard a voice command
those wings away, and felt myself regain
my balance and my calm. I cannot say
exactly how, but felt myself released
and whole again, perhaps. I can't convey
the sense of peace that filled me. Free from pain,
delivered from my fall, I heard your voice

calling to me and wanted to rejoice.
I felt serene and calm, I felt a hushed
tranquility around me, and I knew
all would be well: my agitation ceased
to trouble me. Together, we'd renew
our climb, but now with confidence, unrushed:
I know that voice can guide us past this ground."

Emptiness

My own experience is different: I
may sit in contemplation half the day,
my voice an echoed whispering, until
a silence overtakes me: emptiness
unbroken may mysteriously fill
my heart: stillness becomes a passageway
and leaves room for a quietude that grows

to fill the darkened room, Even time slows
and disappears: my pulse, my spirit rest
until I'm nothing, almost as if death
had taken me. And then, the openness
expands to fill the earth and fill my breath
and I am overcome with blessedness
unbidden and unmerited, a gift

I cannot understand, a sudden shift
of everything I'd known, and all seems clear -
renewed and filled with energy. The long
journey seems short, and filled with quiet bliss
so great my mind is almost filled with song,
and then the things around me reappear
remade, reseen by my transfigured eye.

Candleflame

We found an empty house, completely dark,
and went inside. The entryway was bare
of any decoration. We pushed through
a second door and found another room
completely windowless. There were a few
framed etchings on its walls. We found a stair,
and climbing up, explored the central place

where light from just one candle lit the space.
And in that windless air, the candle burned
with near perfection, endless, unconsumed,
its flame shaped like a swelling lotus bloom
risen above the lake, just now perfumed,
its layered petals opening and turned
towards the sun. The layers of the flame

reformed themselves until each one became
distinct from all the rest and we could see
the separate colors purely: blue and red,
yellow and violet: light pierced the gloom
until its blended colors overspread
the chamber with reflected energy
and from that flame uprose a single spark.

Marriage

She's dressed in layers of reserved brocade,
a belt she's only loosened for my eyes,
whose clasp was my first gift. And underneath
brocade (I know the layers in my heart),
a linen dress, a woven slip to sheath
her skin. And all these layers formalize
her thoughts on love, and mine: we replicate

the greening of the earth and recreate
together, in our unity, the bonds
of roses, interwoven, or the vine
whose labyrinthine tendrils have no start
or end, but seem to disappear, combine
themselves into a figure that responds
to sunlight and to small winds. Energy

surrounds our movements with an ecstasy
of light and love and wind: even her slow
footsteps make me rejoice, and watching her
I celebrate her grace: each studied part,
each layer, separately, may refer
to others, but converged, they seem to glow
with endless luminescence well arrayed.

Cantata

She's singing as we walk. There is no voice
more spirited than hers: it resonates
with passion and with joy on terraces
above, beneath us, echoes off the walls
and makes, of crumbling stonefalls, vortices
of raptured sound. Consonance integrates
the terrace rings together, until each

next level seems more easily in reach,
the walls less steep, the climb less dangerous.
She sings without a score, there is no need
for measure here: her voice rises and falls
without notation, accidentals keyed
into a song growing more rapturous
with every passing step. Listening, I

notice a warm spark falling through the sky:
a brilliant tongue of flame unseen before,
but now spectacular above the stone
marking our path along the waterfalls,
descending down the slope from some unknown
opulent source we cannot yet explore
whose murmurings invite us to rejoice.

Eudaimonia

A tree, growing nearby, thrust down its roots
and held the mountainside intact. The creek
flowed all around it, slowing near the base
as if the water lingered in its shade,
made of itself a mirror to replace
an image of our sky with the oblique,
transformed and reframed undersides of leaves,

transposing everything vision perceives.
And everywhere, through branches, light streamed down,
reflecting off the waters, in a blaze
of luminescence, an arched colonnade
of flame, whose shimmered beauty formed a maze
of brilliant shadows underneath the crown
of branches. As we watched, a gentle wind

induced the light to change itself again:
the branches seemed to dance, a symphony
of motion changing everything we knew.
The interplays of light and water made
our eyes refocus, helped us to renew
even our vision through their harmony,
and let us see the tree's ripening fruits.

Self-control

Along this rockface every cautious tread
must be planned out, each handhold carefully
considered as we move from stone to stone.
Looking ahead, behind, examining
possible paths, each climber moves alone,
brushing away fragments, the rough debris
of earthquakes, and the flaking granite crust,

even when dazzled by the lambent dust.
Sometimes a vein of outworn quartz appears,
provides a ridge to let the climber stand
or walk slantwise along the glistening
rock scarp, well balanced by a single hand
pressed against stone, until the passage clears.
But mostly I must find a cleft and lean

away from the cliff face, moving between
solidity of stone and open air -
the line dividing them hard to define
exactly when the torn sky's darkening
as hollow forms fracture and recombine,
until those clouds, breaking, restore the glare
and we refind our passage overhead.

Gentleness

The next ring held a vineyard, well-designed,
so that the sun in turning overhead
warmed every narrow row in turn, and air
flowed freely through the clustered up-turned leaves.
The stream, diverted, saturated bare
terrain, and stakes allowed the vines to thread
supportive tendrils across trellises,

and interwoven, on rough lattices,
canopies thrived. Some workers moved along
the levelled rows retraining rampant stalks
so that each flourishing branchlet receives
just the right light, projecting the rootstocks'
vibrance upwards, until, crowning, their strong
canes, flowering, unfurl their minute

petals, and swift bees pollinate the fruit.
The rampant fertile clusters must be thinned
by hand, allowing each to fully grow,
and each is bound so rough twine interweaves
with polished stems, until the ripe fruits glow
with their own sweetness, nurtured by this wind
where water, air, and light are all combined.

Goodness

We came upon a man building a frame,
the structure of a house, from lumber sawn
and aged until it dried and every curve
was gone: the wood was stacked, square, true and straight.
We watched him search for the best piece to serve
as the next upright, matching a plan drawn
completely in his mind. It seemed he could

imagine, just by looking, how the wood
would stand after he trimmed it down to length.
He measured every side with a marked stick.
This simple benchmark helped him estimate
the least wastage, a piece too long or thick
was saved for other uses where more strength
would be required: there was more to build.

And yet, no matter how the craftsman's skilled,
there always will be cutoffs, some small waste.
The prudent save these for new purposes,
but even smaller projects generate
their own, in turn. The craftsman focuses
on these, knowing each bevel's soundly placed
until there are no fragments to reclaim.

Patience

We found a field newly harvested,
the empty stalks stubble, already burned.
Small birds explored the broken, stony ground,
flitting from place to place, looking for grain
unnoticed by the harvesters. She found
a few small kernels everywhere she turned
and we together searched for every bit,

believing gathered morsels benefit
in unexpected ways, accumulate,
and when taken together they become
more than we'd hoped. We struggled to retrain
our eyes, refocus vision, overcome
deceptive shadows, tried to concentrate
on single, patterned forms, their husks unfurled.

We need to find new eyes to see the world,
to understand ascending passages,
and read the hidden evidence of earth,
the covert morsels scattered on this plain
may sprout in unknown places, and give birth
to different journeys, other voyages
distinct from sights our eyes interpreted.

Kindness

Our last ascent: the summit within sight.
I lead, she follows. Carefully I choose
each step, not for my stride length, but for hers.
Sometimes I turn, and reaching, take her hand.
This act, in helping her, also confers
on me a sense of freedom, and I lose
my isolation, and the inwardness

that holds us back. Uncompassed openness
infuses me with a new balance, brings
my delicate slow movements new resolve
until the path we'd improvised, unplanned,
seems natural: our obstacles dissolve
until passage seems easy: her voice sings
with a new joy, and from her melody

my spirit resonates in harmony.
The wind has fallen now close to the peak,
and everywhere around, the sound of larks
singing surrounds us, rising from this land
of rock and streams and tongues of flame, their sparks
guiding our journey to the goal we seek
as we ascend towards the warming light.

Peace

The last terrace was smaller than the rest:
a summit and some space. The middle point
was marked by a few rocks, but from those stones
a spring emerged, the water flowing free
from every crevice. Drinking there atones
for all our missteps. She wanted to anoint
my forehead with those waters, and I sensed

through her movements the journey recompensed.
Around us, everywhere, the tongues of flame
hovered like birds, illuminating all,
casting no shadows as their energy
pulsed through us, as we felt even the small
deep tremors of the mountain overcame
our balance and our spirits. Our hearts swelled

with a new peace, reenergized, compelled
to sing, and we two sang with just one voice,
and gazed in transfixed wonder at the scene:
the water, flame, and wind, our ecstasy
beyond the visions each of us had seen
alone, and as we started to rejoice
we felt our journeyed life together blessed.

MEDITATION II

CHARISMATA CANTICLE

"She lives and does not live; a woman of ashes, she perceives and does not perceive; and she reveals the marvels of God not by herself but as one touched by them, just as a string touched by the harper sounds not by itself but by his touch."

~ Saint Hildegard of Bingen

Music Vigil

A man lay dying in a shuttered room,
unconscious, barely breathing, as his wife
sat near him, weeping. Someone whispered prayers
all night, until the unremembered dawn
broke through their darkness. Steps mounted the stairs:
a woman entered as he fought for life.
She crossed herself and then began to sing.

And as the morning sunlight seems to bring
illumination to the forest, fills
what seemed like empty air with energy,
with unsuspected radiances drawn
from somewhere else, almost an ecstasy
of interwoven streams of light, instills
within the wanderer a sudden peace,

just so her voice brought those present release
from weeping and from grief, and in their place
a quiet joy crept in. They wept, but now
their weeping was transfigured in her song:
only spiritual beauty could allow
such transformations, opening to grace,
as rose buds, warmed by dawn, open and bloom.

Intricate Forms Lead to Contemplation

I walk our river's forest every day
and know by heart each pre-established path
beside each bank. The patterns of the trees
are rational: the sycamores along
the riverside need water. Where the breeze
blows stronger in our cloudburst's aftermath,
maples and cherries thrive. I understand

some see in this the tokens of a plan.
And some, who contemplate the beauty in
the patterns of a leaf, ask how they came
into graceful existence, note their strong
resemblances to streams, and wish to name
their unseen cause outright. But I begin
more modestly: I look upon the leaf

and in complexity find some relief
from searching, and then, lost within that gaze,
open myself to things I never knew.
Just so, through contemplation of her song,
I rediscover everything that grew
within the forest, and am moved to praise
even a fallen leaf's patterned array.

Ubi Caritas

She lives within her song, but does not live
outside measures: she sings but does not sing.
She is a lyre played by unseen hands
and if she calms herself, it's to reveal
the energy her spirit understands,
the force only external light can bring.
Her voice's beauty helps us recollect

a deeper beauty, helps us reconnect
with everything we've lost, and yet preserves
our fragile vibrancy: we are too frail
to know resplendence openly, the real
beauty behind the songs: she is a veil,
a shadow on that brilliance, which conserves
our sight for other visions. And if we

can truly hear her music, charity
may be strengthened within us, we may learn
the gentleness of grace and know the sweet
constraints only her measures can unseal,
if only we can share in her complete
surrender to the spirit, if we burn
in that same flame: peaceful, contemplative.

Muérome de Amores, Carillo

A man, languid within his cell, once heard
a worker just outside who sang of pain,
and as the man, inside his darkness, learned
lyrics and melody combined as one,
a flame kindled within him, and he burned
with that same love. He wanted to sustain
the presence he had felt while listening.

This led to his own gift's awakening.
Some say a light illuminated all
the space around him, lit even the air:
as if that flame inside him had begun
to overcome the darkness everywhere,
lighting his desk, the parchment, and the wall
unshadowed, as if light blazed from inside

each object, as if beauty could reside
in everything around him. He began
to write his own songs then, and they became
a different kind of light. The verses spun
like silk, like glass, glowing within the same
internal light, so we could understand
the energy inside each brilliant word.

Bridge Across the River

Fallen branches define our wilderness,
valleys crisscrossed by interrupted streams,
pathways washed out or blocked by fallen limbs,
briars prevent our easy travelling.
Watching a swallow as its wingbeat skims
the water's surface, even smooth flight seems
obstructed everywhere by riverbanks.

Even the bridges have been lost, their planks
washed downstream in a storm. But near one bend
where currents narrow, a large sycamore
has fallen, bank to bank. Its roots still cling
half in the earth, and on the other shore
strong boughs, half-cracked but still alive, suspend
the trunk above the changing water's flow.

It makes a kind of bridge. Small branches grow
upright along its length, and a small rope
provides a means of balancing along
the dappled bark. And if our path, crossing
the stream just here, becomes a cause for song,
it also gives us verdant cause for hope
that we may cross at last to promised bliss.

Ave Maria

The colors of her strong voice interweave,
in mirrors, light and flame, and reconnect
this earth with an eternal realm. Her words
gentle, but filled with force, fall on our ears
like rain, life-giving, or like songs of birds
whose light enraptured harmonies reflect
the peace of every orchard we have known.

And through her voice, chaos is overthrown,
the colors of this earth are harmonized
into a brilliant prism, mirroring
the concord where confusion disappears,
where we, in tranquil unity, can sing
Her blissful praise, in voices crystallized
a moment through the joy Her presence gives.

Her voice, nourished by lucent waters, lives
within us, gathers us, restores our breath,
so we may sing sweet canticles to praise
colors of earth, or music of the spheres,
whose measures teach the numbering of days,
comfort even the hour of our death,
remind us, in our darkness, not to grieve.

Canticle

I've seen no doves or tongues of flame. I've seen
no hurricanes within an enclosed space,
or roses wreathed in snow. And yet, one night,
I knew a moment I cannot explain
by reason or emotion. Candlelight
lit a small church, a consecrated place
of wood and glass. We few had gathered there

to hear an evening's music. Everywhere
around me papers rustled as the strings
of a quartet grew still. And then her voice,
without music behind her, clear and plain,
filled the whole room. It caused us to rejoice
and weep at once, as if each time she sings,
in opening herself, through grace and skill,

she opens us, as if she could instill,
in everyone who hears, love's harmony.
Is she a mirror of the spirit or
an opaque luminescent windowpane
hinting at passages? Does she restore,
within her voice's beauty, ecstasy
we thought we'd lost: transcendent, blessed, serene?

This Is How a Person Becomes a Flowering Orchard

Out of the earth itself, out of the stones,
out of the fertile soil waiting here,
unbundled cuttings root, and sprout their leaves.
At first tender, at first uncertain, their
new growth seems emerald. Each stem receives
water and nutrients, and if kept clear
of weeds will rise and branch, become a tree.

But still the seasons grant no certainty:
locusts may chew the leaves or deer may strip
the winter bark. But if the trunk survives,
the verdant leaves will thrive in April air,
supporting every blossom that arrives,
and all the energetic bees who slip
between petals, performing their minute

dances for pollen, fertilizing fruit.
Each humble action, small and commonplace,
is multiplied by others and, transformed,
becomes a verse within a larger prayer
if through the summer every branch is warmed
by sunlight flowing over limbs like grace,
until autumn reveals jewel tones.

Robe of Beauty

We wrap ourselves within her robe of song,
woven of harmony and gathered light,
as if she drew into herself the flame
swirling through all of us and could sustain
in song its energy, and overcame
stillness and quietude through her delight
in beauty. She is the Spirit's harp, who weaves

through her, comfort to everyone who grieves,
but even more: her joyful singing veils
brightness surrounding us, which otherwise
would dazzle us to blindness, and constrain
our sight to shadows. As our voices rise
with hers, a deeper form of sight prevails,
lit by a living flame: she is the lyre

who unifies, through hymns, water and fire
to soothe our souls and light our path. The grace
within her song allows us to explore
the golden threads connecting this domain
to greater permanence, as if a door,
opened by song, allowed us to retrace
our path, and find the place where we belong.

Cien Ovejas

My eyesight must be failing. I can see
within the polished surfaces of stone
reflected scenes: the altar stairs, the long
diffuse reflection of rose windows, blue
and red across the marble. As her song
continues, unfamiliar lyrics, known
to every other listener, appear:

recurrent, universal, simple, clear.
But how can I, bewildered, understand
the messages her sweet cantata brings,
follow the parable, or know the true
meaning of allegories her voice sings?
How can I see the quiet pastureland
without grasping the simplest turn of phrase?

The answer's in reflections: songs of praise
gain universal beauty in her voice,
and something of the lyric's truth resides
within her melodies. Their meanings grew
as clear as images glazed stone provides
the more I listened, making me rejoice
through contemplation of this mystery.

Mariposa

The jewelled wings in motion intersect
sunlight descending through the forest's shade
for just an instant, disappear to dark.
But if I wait with patience, they return
dancing along the trunks, the mottled bark
of dappled sycamores, blossoms arrayed
along the riverbank, grown almost still,

and if I remain calm, master my will,
relearn serenity, and fix my gaze
across the shore, those motions, jubilant,
remake themselves, in luminescence burn,
continuously flashing in a slant
of sunlight through the canopy, and blaze
across the flowered meadow. They remind

my spirit to rejoice in unconfined
small miracles: even the lightest wings
may be borne up by winds we cannot see,
transported past the flower and the fern
above the woodland's quiet secrecy,
as when, from silent shadows, a voice sings
of how those wings and light interconnect.

Shekhinah

The air is veiled when she sings, lamp light
obscured, as if a cloud descending here
surrounds both her and us, and reunites
song and the wind in shadowed ecstasy.
The simple beauty of her song delights
our spirits, but beyond joy, in the clear
halftones we find a dwelling place. Her song

remakes the wind, persuades us we belong
within its warmth a moment. In her prayer
we hear a call to co-create the earth,
in unison to reinvent beauty.
And in our works we reaffirm the worth
of everything around us: what the air
transfigures in its rising warmth, the flow

of candlesmoke, the backlit afterglow
we hear within her pauses, as the still
excited air prepares itself to bear
the resonant complex simplicity
which clouds and clarifies, leaves us aware
that even patterns of her voice fulfill
the invocation, and restore our sight.

Panis Angelicus

Leaves falling in the forest: who will mourn
for each of them, for any? And for those
of us who fall, light failing, who will sing
the songs we loved, the verses we adored,
and sing them without weeping? Who will bring
sweet joyful expectations to repose
and ease the suffering of those who miss

the ecstasy of passage, reminisce
instead on transitory works and days,
forgetting what we'd hoped for? I have seen
a thousand faces, marked by unexplored
anguish, despair, transformed by the serene
first strains of just her voice lifted in praise:
Ave Maria, Lux Aeterna, lines

invoking grief her jewelled voice refines
into a form of golden joy. Those eyes
which had been weeping take on luminance
and, after several verses, are restored
to clear sight through her graceful consonance,
and turning upward, reaffirm the wise
lyrics her measured harmonies adorn.

Aqua de Vida

At dawn the forest's garlands, wreathed in haze,
open themselves to sunlight and renew
through warmth their living presence. In their green
turnings upward in sequence, they extend
the life of all surrounding things. The scene
is filled with energy, beneath the blue
stillness, the canopy now filled with wings.

And from the mountainside, the hidden springs
which flowed all night, provide a visible
witness of continuity, dissolve
into the earth and, taken up, transcend
their limitations. Sunflowers revolve,
tracking their source, moving, intangible,
but definite within the morning sky.

And we, like them, are summoned to reply,
open ourselves to light warming us all,
refiguring that energy, remake
its fire into song that may ascend
above clear streams, across green leaves, and shake
even the canopy, as if a small
light wind became a hurricane of praise.

Another Kind of Beauty

The boundaries of experience dissolve
in contemplation of the beautiful.
In opening ourselves to song, we gain
passage to unsuspected realms, explore
the mysteries of faith we can't explain,
and meditating on the bountiful
sweet harmonies surrounding us, we hear

echoes of presence. Listening to clear
reinvocations of lost radiance,
we understand the miracles of grace
within our lives, and focusing, restore
our peaceful compositions. There's a trace
of paradise in every voice, brilliance
we almost cannot bear, but if we pause

a moment to receive it, music draws
our spirits to eternal love, we learn
to rediscover everything we've known,
and re-envision the resplendent core
glowing within us all, a warmed gemstone,
and through our works of music, we return
gifts we've received, and help this realm revolve.

The One Breath

Silence in candlelight. Red incense burns
in stillness, and the swirling smoke is caught
in columns made of warmed encompassed air.
She walks towards the center, pauses, waits,
and draws a single breath, inclined to prayer,
so motionless it seems her figure's wrought
from marble or from flowing bronze, but she,

the focus of this earth's vitality
for just this moment, lifts her voice and sings.
How can the formless air, remade to sound,
possess such beauty? Her voice recreates
the harmony we'd thought we'd lost, or found
only in dreams or visions darkness brings
and each dawn banishes. But even here

in this shared place, those visions reappear
or we recover something else. Our breath
flows in with hers: the universe seems one,
united in that beauty, as if gates,
once closed, had been reopened and the sun
flowed once again through gardens, where no death
is mournful, where an endless fire burns.

Fountain

We work our gardens as we can, provide
fountains for irrigation, channels, ponds,
hoping these watercourses irrigate
each corner of our verdant terraces,
believing tended cuttings may create
desired fruits, and that each leaf responds
to water in a flourishing domain.

And yet we long for something else, for rain
to fall unbidden as a kind of gift
beyond our artificial laboring,
replenishing impoverished surfaces
our efforts could not reach, and watering
even neglected roots that, nourished, lift
unearthly petals blooming everywhere.

But there is something more: if we prepare
ourselves through contemplative openness
waters may flow directly to our heart
until the spreading cascade replaces
all dryness in us. So beauty imparts
within its course a spiritual bliss
beyond those fruits our efforts had supplied.

Lorica of St. Patrick

They chanted lyrics as they walked along
the darkened roads, the forested pathways
then filled with unknown dangers, reaffirmed
shaken belief, through repetition held.
They whistled past graveyards. Breastplates confirmed
the very strength they questioned- they would praise
even the shadowed valley fields they crossed.

We understand. And yet something was lost
within those words. In calling out for strength,
they missed sustaining visions, since the strong
casts out the subtle, always. They upheld
outer appearances, but in their song,
which helped them cross the darkened canyon's length,
they overlooked unfathomable gifts.

All wish them well. But as our focus shifts
towards other invocations, some believe
we need to reimagine how we sing
and beauty's real worth: we are compelled
to understand what other voices bring
or how sweet harmonies may interweave
the elements of vision into song.

Epithalamium

Requested by the young bride, she arrives
just as the crowded ceremony starts,
crosses herself, and pauses, focusing.
The calmness of her voice imparts a peace
the couple hadn't known, and her song brings
a blissful consolation to our hearts.
Their lives are filled with beauty. As the white

veil is lifted to the groom's delight,
so her voice lifts the veil from our souls,
and promises a graceful unity.
The Psalm, Sanctus and Gloria increase
the careful prayers of shared community.
The balance of her melody consoles
even the timorous, illuminates

their vows, and after silence, recreates
a sense of harmony as lilies bloom,
and the young bride places flowering gifts
at Mary's feet. The songs offer release
and spread tranquility when her voice lifts
in loving praise, as both the bride and groom
turn to each other, entering their lives.

The Inner Light of Blossoms

It's hard to see in daylight, since the sun
so brightly overpowers everything,
but if we walk at dusk or rise at dawn,
we may discover radiance surrounds
each blooming rose, as if the light were drawn
from somewhere deep within, and glimmering
illuminates even the shadowed air.

And so with her: the lyrics seem to flare
across the congregation, lighting all
with wonder from within, transporting each
to unimagined places, past the bounds
of learned experience, beyond the reach
of everything they'd known. Her songs enthrall,
and free, at once, their spirits, to explore

what they had only dimly seen before:
the light within themselves, ethereal
but tangible, and deep within, the source
they share with her. The beauty of those sounds
is theirs as well, they join without remorse,
discovering, through song, spiritual
communion as their voices merge to one.

Via Pulchritudinis

Some say we should abandon everything:
reject the beauties of this earth, disdain
jewels and silk in homage, and despise
all ornament: 'the simplest path is best'
since any image, pleasing to our eyes,
distracts and cannot help us to maintain
our constant focus on inclusive praise.

Why, then, were forms created? Should we gaze
on flowing waterfalls without delight
and find no joy in patterns of the earth?
Should our creative gifts be dispossessed?
Do they not honor in their humble worth
their origins in half-forgotten light?
Are we not called to co-create beauty?

And so with her: within her melody,
if we're observant, we may find a spark
kindled in distant times, a subtle clue
of sound from vanished gardens, peaceful, blessed
by harmonies reflected in the true
harmonics of her song: her voice's arc
reminds us of a flowing crystal spring.

Claritatis

Light moves as unformed image, and the glass
receives its clarity, capturing still
appearances and figures our own eyes
can only see within the mirror's frame.
This is the gift each looking glass supplies:
allowing sight to linger and distill
the unsuspected elements of forms.

And so with her: in singing she performs
a mirror's work, gathering energy
from everything around, from breath, and she
reflects the figure of the living flame,
not as an image, but as perfectly
translated song. Her graceful melody
remakes what she received, as she breathes out

the beauty of the canticle's devout
continuation, as she moves through time
along the turning pathway of her voice.
And we, in listening, follow the same
pathway with her, she helps us to rejoice
through beauty she reflects, and helps us climb
the same slope she ascends: our true compass.

Rhapsody

This woodland path I follow twists and turns
as it follows the curving river's course,
but sometimes, when the stream is running straight
along the leaf-strewn valley floor, I see
a longer way ahead, and speculate
about the distant goal, the river's source
in hills or mountains I have never seen.

But thinking of such goals neglects the green
vibrance around me: how the apple boughs
hide jewelled fruit beneath their changing leaves.
I know the flowing river seeks the sea,
gathering strength as each stream interweaves
its waters with the rest, how light allows
our eyes to map its path, but for my own

I have no guide. The hidden birds intone
unending beauty in their songs, provide
directions through the flashing of their wings,
as if nature's composite rhapsody
lived fully within air, and each voice brings
its culmination to this riverside,
while in each leaf an endless fire burns.

Coloratura

We could not bear the light directly, so
it streams through a rose window, gold and green,
and sometimes passes through a pane left clear,
cascading through the faceted sapphire
her ring holds while she sings. And as we hear
the colors of her voice, the darkened scene
is lit with iridescent prismed light.

The charismatic measures dazzle sight
in harmony with sound: we contemplate
the facets of her voice, how they recall
remembered tones. A luminescent lyre,
she gathers to herself even the small
currents of air, the hues that recreate,
combined within her song, a light that seems

moved by the wind. The glowing prism streams
and flows though air around us, dazzling
our souls to stillness. Through her we embrace
a tranquil energy, the living fire
that blazes through her voice, and we retrace
those currents, beauty's centered offering:
through her clear lights, small winds, calm waters flow.

Charismata

Her voice gives energy, her voice invites
parishioners at dawn to celebrate
the mysteries of spirit, and remind
themselves of beauty's gifts. Each, drawn to Mass,
remembers something hidden, the refined
lost understandings her songs recreate,
and find the earth refigured and remade

within a simple song. Her voice may fade
and yet they carry with them, through the day,
not just her song, but everything they'd lost
and found through her, as if a looking glass
could hold an image, as if light, embossed
on mirrors, could remain, a bright array
of patterns serving as a lucent guide.

But more than this: her songs, reheard, provide
a hint of grace through beauty, reconnect
the blossom and what drives its opening,
encourages each petal to surpass
its limitations: as we hear her sing,
we each are overcome by the direct
experience of all her voice unites.

Be the Mirror of Life in the Eyes of the Dove

We walk the riverwood and celebrate
the beauty of this earth, the vibrant leaves,
birdsong whose unseen source is hidden by
a thousand fruits and flowers. We delight
in every aspect of the azure sky,
uniting all creative sight perceives:
the forms of clouds, the vigor of the wind.

But in our exaltation, we begin
to mirror all we see, wish to reframe
that beauty with our hands, and reinvent
those images that move us, and rewrite
the patterns of the wind, the slow ascent
of song or smoke, as if a hidden flame
warmed everything around us, and renewed

the hidden songs our ecstasies pursued,
the half-heard messages we understand
within our hearts and struggle to express
with our own words. Our voices reunite
both wind and leaf, and through them, we possess
reflections of that beauty and expand
the green boundaries of life we recreate.

Viriditas

Expect no voices. Do not look for words
written in blazing letters on the sky
or chiseled into granite on your wall.
Do not assume visions will pierce your sight
or any of your senses. There's no thrall
compelling you, or making things comply
with what you've known. Open yourself, and know

without knowing the source. Allow the flow
to fill you silently, until your heart
can understand, remember, and renew
in your own words, shadows of living light,
bringing to others the same peace that grew
within your spirit. If those words impart
the same tranquility, then you may learn

to trust their source, and trust in their return.
Notice, especially, the way their green
ardor infuses everything. Around
the new space you inhabit, watch the bright
roses thriving in once resistant ground
and opening themselves, until the scene
is rich with rose perfume and flashing birds.

Feather

A single dove flew in the opened door,
perching among church rafters while she sang
Ave Maria as the incense rose,
and as small candles warmed the rising air.
The beauty of her song seemed to transpose
the mourners' grief to joy as her voice rang
across the perfumed air, seemed to enthrall

and calm each listener. Just then, a small
feather, perhaps a fringe of down, began
to float above their heads, light as a breath,
light as the verses of a whispered prayer
half-murmured at the moment of our death.
The feather rose gently above the span
of central beams, and gracefully returned,

moved by an unseen force. A small flame burned
within an oil lamp: perhaps it warmed
spirals of air and drove the quill along
smoothed columns as it drifted everywhere?
I cannot say. I only know her song
rose with the feather's movements, and transformed
by unseen energy, appeared to soar.

Reflection

Her voice weaves light, her measures interlace
the flowing streams of colors and of sound.
In comforting the moment of our death
with serene beauty, she provides a way
of passage, a release: cascades of breath
flow though her as her harmonies surround
our centered luminescence, mirroring

another half-remembered offering.
In opening ourselves, we recreate
the beauty we reflect, the living flame
burning through us, whose faceted array
prisms and glows within the jeweled frame
of whispered song, and lets us contemplate
the peace her voice restores, the harmony

unveiled through her crystal rhapsody.
Her singing recreates the blossoming
of gardens all around us, and sustains
the focused joy within us, helps us pray
along with her. In beautiful refrains
we find our center, and in opening
our ears to song, open our hearts to grace.

MEDITATION III

BROTHER SUN, SISTER MOON

Let the heavens be glad and the earth rejoice;
let the sea and what fills it resound;
let the plains be joyful and all that is in them.
Then let all the trees of the forest rejoice

~ Psalm 96:11-12

"They have pierced My hands and My feet,
they have numbered all My bones."

~ Prayer Before a Crucifix

Dedicated to Robert Michael Lantry and Mother Miriam Rose Niethus, VHM

Correspondence

My Brother Sun, my dearest Sister Moon,
the two who taught me in my youth, I swore
to write you of my journey. I've been lax,
so please forgive me as I write you now,
recounting here the disappearing tracks
of my long path towards a distant shore
you could not know. Now share with me in verse

this rocky track the fearful may traverse
only with aid, the guidance of a hand
unseen but felt. Be with me as I pass
the mile-markers daylight will allow
deciphering, the moonlit weather-glass
predicting how the rain-shadows will stand
against the distant peaks, which seem more near

whenever our wind blows horizons clear.
I am as lost as any man, but take
one step after another, moving towards
some unknown hidden orchard, where a bough
hangs heavy with sweet fruit, and gentle chords
of wind-composed music, played for our sake,
fulfill morning's promise in afternoon.

The Relinquishing

Dear Brother, I acquired everything
I thought I needed for the desert, packed
each item carefully in its own space,
and lifted up the burden of my gear.
I staggered from its weight. With little grace
I set out walking. Traversing the cracked
red brittle earth, I hoped only for shade

and followed ancient paths water had made.
Resting, I reconsidered what I bore,
and with each pause, left something small behind.
A tiny gift of food for roaming deer,
small metal vessels roadrunners might find
attractive, even flaskets meant to store
sufficient water for a couple days -

I left them all to warm in the sun's rays.
And I felt lighter, or perhaps my strength
was growing: which of these, I can't decide.
I only know the pathway now seemed clear,
walking felt easier with every stride,
and near sunset when shadows grew in length
I camped beside a flowing desert spring.

Calibrations

Sister, my father owned an aging car
an Austin-Healy Sprite, which constantly
broke down along the roadside. Then he said
"Let's take it all apart, and build it back
with new pistons and valves." That day, we spread
a sheet out on the shop floor. By degree
I'd place the bolts in order, then expose

the next part, till he said "now unscrew those
four bolts." I turned the steel socket wrench
not understanding anything but trust.
He taught me how to calibrate, to pack
grease into bearings, how to sand off rust.
He taught me how to organize a bench
so I could find the tools I might need,

and how careless motions could make me bleed,
how every work brought forth a little blood,
and showed me how the part I had ignored
was critical, how to reduce the slack
of fanbelts, watching closely as I poured
the oil, so the crankcase wouldn't flood,
and how to calibrate a torsion bar.

Recessional

Brother, you did not come to see me leave.
I left alone. The jetplane, silver, rose.
And from its windows I looked on my home
a last time, from a distant point of view.
The mountains leading down to white sea foam,
the desert where agaves interpose
their thorns with flame: all faded from my eyes

as we moved through the oceanic skies.
I landed in a foreign place: the rain
grew too familiar quickly, so I fled
on railroads south: reverberating through
the legendary vineyards, frost-burnt, dead.
And then, when I awoke, the bullet train
had made Provence: where red grape clusters still

hung from long vines creeping along the hill
as the sun rose. I thought of you, and how
you would delight before this vision, know
the names of vines, perhaps explain the blue
reflections of the Mistral sea, bestow
on beauty all our human words allow,
where vines, red earth, and azure interweave.

From La Brigue

Sister, in Seaside Alps, the paved road ends
at Notre Dame des Fountains, a small church
outside La Brigue. I spent a few weeks there
midsummer gazing on frescos restored
in our own times. Abrasive mountain air
has scrubbed some walls to blankness, but research
and patience brought back others. Beautiful

visions of passion and the merciful
garlands depicted there reward our gaze
until we face the western wall. Behind
some curtains, hidden, Giovanni poured
his worst moments in plaster, as his mind
escaped, or all his fears consumed his days.
Devoured by strange beings, ruined souls

are torn and bleeding, pressed between the scrolls
of rigid letters. I rejected these,
preferring, in my mind, beatitudes,
the Spirit lifting me until I soared
through pure wind where no suffering intrudes
beyond those granite ridges, past forked trees
above the dreadful scenes beauty transcends.

From Isola 2000

Brother, the skiing slopes look almost groomed
from up here on the lift. The winter sky
is cold and clear. What's distant seems so near!
This separation seems a simple span,
easily bridged. And though it may appear
these mountain ridges, rising, multiply
as I ascend, I know the continent

is limited. The oceans represent
only a mental barrier, my words
could fly in days to you. But could you know
the burden underneath them? As I scan
the sheer rockfaces overhung with snow,
I think of deserts, brittlebush, small birds
perched deep inside the manzanita's shade,

and as I ponder them, they seem to fade.
The distances are farther than we think,
our steps labored. Snowdrifts rising above
my head block passage, overwhelm my plan.
I've lost the vision of a desert dove
who flutters towards a creek, hoping to drink.
All streams are frozen here, nothing has bloomed.

Note from Paradise

Dear Sister, I've found paradise. It dwells
somewhere in hinterlands above Marseille,
a little east of Aix. Crafted in stone,
a farmhouse there has stood for centuries,
facing an ancient cross. I went alone
to visit friends by invitation, pray
and rest. But who can rest when such work calls:

the maintenance of whispered waterfalls,
the sibilance of irrigation streams
which must be cleared after each passing storm?
We labored every morning. Work is ease
when done in joy. And when the sun grew warm,
we rested in the orchard's shade. It seems
sunlight reflected through the waving leaves

can light all earth, and us, as it reweaves
our bonds to every soul who has walked here.
And in the evening, trout from the pond
suffice for dinners rich enough to please
our simple hungers, whose needs correspond
to our day's work as fireflies appear,
and in the verdant orchard nightbreeze swells.

Great Silence

Brother, the work consumes. I read. I write.
A rosary is wrapped around my wrist.
Sometimes in conversations, I discern
hints of eternal words in daily speech
and then, in silent contemplation, learn
how even in great silence words persist
through pure and subtle clarity. I rest

in harmony when thoughts have coalesced,
and then I write again, hoping to hold
complexities in ordered disarray
in honor of the song that moves through each
of us in turn. It takes most of the day.
I have been known to shiver in the cold
even in summer when the air grows still,

but have a blissful devoir to fulfill.
At evening, I rest. The village crowds
swirl through an animation I can't match.
I find respite along the stone-paved beach,
and after sunset watch the dories catch
fish in arclights, as alabaster clouds
rush back shorewards to populate our night.

One Song

Sister, I found a house in St. Pancrace.
The rent was almost nothing, but it meant
I had to walk each morning to the ville
through cherry orchards, vineyards, down switchbacks
cutting through olive groves. When winds were still,
I felt the birds companion my descent:
they shared my terraced journey to the sea

providing a symphonic company.
But in the evening, or after dark,
the uphill journey lengthened. I would hold
my staff at ready against boar attacks
that never came. Bracing against the cold,
I listened to the fox's cry, the bark
of feral dogs roaming through the wood,

speaking in tongues I nearly understood.
I hear them now, in memory, the long
abandoned cries against the darkness, held
a note too long, echoed above the tracks
we both had made, as if we were compelled
by spirit or terrain to sing one song
as we danced, separately, through vineyard grass.

From the Baie des Anges

We came across a woman sitting outside
in deep sunlight, with coiled ropes nearby,
each knotted hopelessly. She would take one,
examine it, and hold it up to light,
knowing somewhere she'd see a hint of sun,
and that small hint might help her hands untie
or loosen, just a bit, the tangled strain.

She worked a little, held it up again,
and worked a little more. But each one held
a twisted knot too dense for human hands
to unplait: too contorted, pulled too tight.
For these she used a metal spike: the bands
would give way. Her dexterity compelled
their opening, and searching, she would find

a pathway that might lead her to unbind,
with gentle artistry, each hidden knot.
Once done she stretched each rope to its whole length
then, splicing carefully, she'd reunite
each to the longer whole, restore the strength
it held within itself when it was wrought
before misworking let it become tied.

Consolation

Sister, some nights are filled with nameless things–
shadows, or something else: I watch them crawl
chaotic near the corners, and contend
with unseen obstacles, while my own eyes,
half dazzled in the lamplight, comprehend
nothing within their patterns on the wall,
no purpose any mortal could discern,

except that, deep within them, fires burn.
Are these the same flames blazing in our souls,
some universal energy that dwells
in every living, breathing thing that flies
or walks along a path? Our breathing swells
or blazes up, and that strange light consoles
our wonder or our fears, reminds us then

of how the gentle dawn will come again.
Something I can't articulate remains
with me all night, a presence close at hand.
I call it light, but no word could comprise
its consolation, who could understand
the luminescence radiance contains?
I only know the comfort its warmth brings.

At Chartres

Brother, I went to Chartres and wept for you,
for me, for all of us. I was the last
admitted for the day, when our late sun
slanted across rose windows, so the blue
changed light transfigured every brace, and spun
moving impressions overhead, or cast
deep shadows into every aperture,

and yet that transformed light seemed clear and pure.
I wandered through stone forests, labyrinths
beneath my feet, and gazed at emptiness
above my head: the open spaces grew
more complex as they rose, as if to bless,
in juxtapose, the squared-off humble plinths
of fluted columns, rising till they find

themselves supporting arches redefined.
I felt alone among them, I felt lost,
as if my voice were nothing when compared
to finished stones, each chiseled, square and true,
by unknown hands, faces discreetly flared,
and placed sequentially, until they've crossed,
bringing their hidden structure into view.

A Tongue of Fire

Sister, I summon words. I speak the names
of objects in my reach, table or chair,
things I can see, and what remains unseen:
the presences I felt in ecstasy
or recollect through shadows on a screen
backlit by candlelight, whose sudden flare
suggests an open window. When I turn,

words on my lips, the candle starts to burn
a little lower once again. I know
the edges of our visions indicate
all we had missed when most we tried to see.
And when we spin, figures regenerate
at those new edges of our sight, the slow
encompassing of patterns, recognized

only in reconstructions, undisguised.
And so with words: we grasp only a hint
of what lies underneath them, what they store
within their portals, the periphery
of echoes, shadowed names that might restore
some understanding to us, as the glint
on polished edges reflects candleflames.

The Shared Path

Brother, I stand in shadows gently cast
by mountain ridges, buildings, and these trees
I cannot name, lifting their branches out
almost into the paths of birds, who spin
through light I cannot reach, and dance about
as if they hear the sacred melodies
some say are all around us. Dusk descends,

the voices still, until each shadow blends
with every other and the colonnades
are silent. In this moment I can sense
the boundaries of our journeys growing thin
as if my path were yours, and this intense
fervor of single destination fades.
My path is yours: you are the one who stands

gazing through darkness in these foreign lands,
and I am on your path, where junipers
withstand the desert sun. And this complete
moment contains all others: now within
my heart your blood is pulsing, and the sweet
birdsongs I heard echo in soft whispers,
their harmonies of stillness unsurpassed.

Lavender Blossoms

Sister, simplicity my only gift,
I humbly write you as I pause to rest.
I carry you with me, within my mind,
describing foreign sights in honest terms
as if your ears could hear. Now, unconfined
by any wall or forest, dispossessed
of any goal, I walk through countryside

with nothing but a falcon's flight to guide
my unplanned steps. In seams of wind-shaped hills,
low stands of lavender are blossoming,
their delicate aroma reaffirms
the cycled beauty of abandoning
direction, since the wild fragrance fills
each valley equally. Near every bend

or every broken talus I descend,
some new blossom awaits. I give them names,
imagining my words could somehow match
their forms, imagining my path confirms
that falcon's flight, whose wings, extended, catch
each breeze, and whose excited voice proclaims
the joy of rising mistrals, smooth and swift.

Water of Life

Brother, I found some shelter in a cave
cleft deep into a hillside where the earth
opened before me. Walking in I found
pictures, carvings, the relics of an age
I hadn't known or guessed. On that damp ground
the scattered, broken images of birth
and loss were everywhere, and drew me on

deeper into the darkness, as if drawn
by something inside me. There was a trace
of incense in the air, the residue
of gathered herbs: vanilla grass and sage?
And farther in, the narrow passage grew
much larger, opened out into a space
lit from above. In silence I explored

the deepest passage, where a clear spring poured
its waters forth, which pooled and disappeared
almost at once into the porous stone.
I drank its sweetness hoping to assuage
the thirst driving me on, secrets half-known,
half-guessed by ancient artists who revered
something beyond what their perceptions gave.

Whirlpool

Sister, a mountain pool called to me.
I folded all my garments and walked in,
wading into its swirled waters, cold
and warm at once, as if its currents swelled
from different sources, vibrant, uncontrolled.
Around my limbs those waters seemed to spin
in dancing vortices. What hand could start

such motions? Or what hidden strength impart
to unmistakably transparent streams
such balanced forces? I can only say
I walked in their intensity, compelled
to each new step. The streambank fell away:
I had to swim out where the surface gleams
with scattered light. And then I was pulled down

an instant. Panicked, thinking I might drown,
or simply disappear, I tried to rise
but could not move, and so I just let go,
drifting through vortices. A current welled
beneath me, bore me up, patient and slow,
until I felt the air, opened my eyes,
and found myself able to truly see.

Fisherman

Brother, low branches hung above streambanks.
I had to bend in passing, had to lean
out over rushing waters to get past,
to find a place to stand. My fishing pole
kept getting caught: I had no room to cast,
and yet I felt great gratitude, serene,
peaceful, as if the heart of that small stream

were my own heart. I'd seen the flickered gleam
of trout holding the current, gauging flow,
rising and falling as the waters turned
back on themselves, till each part seemed a whole,
and each drop, leaping into air, returned
back to the stream meandering below
in its own time. I watched the swallows flit

and circle along surfaces sunlit
by the last rays of that long afternoon,
and when their wings moved on I cast my fly.
The patient waiting calmed my restless soul.
And so I lingered, even as the sky
grew dark above me, since I knew the moon
would light my path along the mountain's flanks.

Interior Melodies

Sister, night-walking above timberline
I saw the granite glisten in moonlight
as if alive, and felt new gratitude.
I paused to watch the quartz-veins scintillate,
as if the moon's translucent glow renewed
something within each crystal, or my sight,
so dimmed before, had undergone a change,

so I could see their structures, rich and strange.
While constellations turned above my head
and cloudless wind moved silently along,
I paused beneath that ridge to contemplate
stillness and motion, how a single song
can capture both at once, and overspread
like stars, our earth, and through its measures spin

exterior reflections deep within
internal melodies we each can hear
if we can only listen to the sounds
we'd missed, whose harmonies reverberate
within us all, whose resonance surrounds
our movements, until all elements appear
in balance underneath a single sign.

Intertwined Light

Brother, I am the incense and the smoke,
the burning flame, the wick, the candlewax.
I am the leaf, detached, blown on the breeze
above these mountain ridges where the sun
warms everything at once: the redbark trees,
the purple fruit of vines and the blue flax
from which skilled hands make robes: we wear the earth,

unknowing, from the moment of our birth.
Skyclad, stream-draped, we move as water falls,
seeking a place where every current stills,
the pattern finished and the weaving done.
We sing the streambanks and we sing the hills
and they sing us: each ridge, each valley calls
in its own voice, whose beauty intertwines

with every other song, as tendriled vines
weave through each other, raising everything
towards the light. We rise together, lift
each separate drop till banks are overrun
and all becomes a single flowing gift
whose energy inspires us to sing
with every sound we've heard since we awoke.

From Three Islands

Sister, I found a mountain lake, whose banks
could not be seen- they disappeared in mist,
and on the shoreline found a small canoe
as if it had been placed there just for me.
I pushed out from the sands, and as I drew
the paddle backwards, pushed down with my wrist
and watched the vortices spin back towards land.

Ahead, on the first island, a rough stand
of willows wept, their branches bent, their leaves
cascading to the earth. And on the next
the cottonwoods shed down. It floated free
on every breath of wind. I almost blessed
its changing beauty, since each wing receives
a unique beam of sunlight, but each ray

has the same source. They left a passageway
to the next island, where tall sycamores
held up the sky with mottled trunks. Each place
had its own beauty. Vibrant ecstasy
pulsed through them all, and yet they made one space:
a single basin where the sunlight pours
like grace onto each pilgrim giving thanks.

Dark Night

Brother, the path grew hard. In my descent
I lost my way. The trail was unmarked:
on broken granite slabs scattered with scree
no track survives. Sunlight fractured the stone,
knife edges fringed each crevice. By degree
the slope grew steeper as the daylight arced
from every prismed surface. As I crossed

each precipice, I counted up the cost
of just one misplaced step. There was no bridge-
I had to leap from slab to slab. And when
I looked behind, I knew I was alone
in that harsh place, arid, sterile, barren.
I forced myself to move along the ridge,
but when I found no further way, I stopped.

On all three sides, the sheer rock faces dropped
a thousand feet: there was no moving on
and no way back, the mountain was too steep.
I fell into the worst despair I've known,
and in my solitude, began to weep.
I stayed there all that night, and in the dawn
attempted the impossible ascent.

From the Edge

Sister, the light no longer found my eyes.
I made my way in darkness, though the sun
lit everything around me. Climbing blind
I reached above my head to grasp each ledge
and pulled my body up. I was resigned
to trust whatever guided me, to shun
my own uncertain tremblings, and be led

by something deep within my heart instead.
I heard a voice I couldn't understand,
or felt it, without words, inside my brain.
I knew it would not lead me to the edge
or leave me there surrounded by my pain.
I knew, whatever came, I could withstand
if only I could listen, so I moved

as slowly as I dared along the grooved
faultlines of broken stone. My weak hands slipped,
all strength had left my limbs. Yet I still heard
that quiet voice within, which let me pledge
to keep moving, without a spoken word,
and freed from my uncertainty, I gripped
the last handhold which, conquered, let me rise.

Last Journey

Brother, although I'm blind, yet I can see
your last journey from here. I know you left
whatever you had cherished on a shelf
and walked into the daylight, turning west.
The pain you knew that day I've felt myself:
our solitude, our emptiness, bereft
of any comfort, any of the sweet

voices of hidden birds. You walked the street
or we walked it together, till you found
the forest's edge. And still you walked. The grove
was comforting, although its shadows pressed
darkness upon you, dappled light that wove
a web to trap your heart. There was no sound
to reach your ears: our words were left unsaid,

and when the evening came your spirit fled.
The shadows disappeared. The desert breeze
stopped moving, as it does when the sun sets.
No nightingales sang you to your rest,
only the moonlight burnished those secrets
we carried in our hearts through the dark trees
while longing for a final harmony.

The Twisted Knot

Sister, these bones are numbered. All this pain
is poured out, as a broken vessel pours
its contents, all at once, out through the cracks.
And these glazed eyes, half sightless, still convey
the harrowed images of barren tracks.
Their shadowed intimation underscores
the silence I know now. There is a knot

tied deep within me. All the peace I'd sought
seems caught within rosettes of ligaments
twisted and torn somewhere within my heart.
The words I once heard clearly fade away.
The columns of my sanctuary start
to shatter, and their serrated fragments
tear at my skin until my hands are red

with all the useless blood my wounds have shed.
I would cry out and yet I have no voice,
no words to speak, and no way to untie
this knot twisting my heart, constricted, gray
as any sunless dawn, when the blank sky,
uncircumscribed, gives no cause to rejoice
but overwhelms us with remorseless rain.

Rustic Cross

Brother, we walked in silence to the place
of your last rest. There was no wall, no fence,
no gated sanctuary, just bare ground
in which rough junipers were rooted, strong
against the desert light. And all around
the wind was swirling red dust, evidence
of our shared passages. A rustic cross

made only of bound sticks signaled our loss.
Your name and dates carved roughly on one wing,
obscured already by the ochre dust,
seemed transient, as if they'd soon belong
to no-one here. But when a desert gust
moved across sand, a sudden shimmering
dazzled my vision. Then, somehow, I knew

I bore you in my heart. I carried you
in every word I spoke, in every phrase,
and your blood in my veins renewed my strength.
It helped me stand. Someone began a song.
I measured emptiness against its length,
but through those measures, I was filled with praise,
and whispered: "Hail Mary, full of grace…"

Untier of Knots

Sister, the tiny flowers at my feet,
scarlet and rose, open their petals wide
wherever dawn light touches them. They turn
with me towards the sunlight in the east,
as the same rose and scarlet seems to burn
across the early sky. The knot untied
inside my heart opens like those small buds,

until a healing correspondence floods
through every part of me. I praise the day,
the birdsongs and the winds, the flowing streams
renewing this parched land. Even the least
small fluttering of swallowtails seems
as graceful as an elegant ballet:
the earth dances around us. And what drives

the radiance around us, what survives
through grief and joy? Who can untie the cords
that bind us to the earth, or to our pain?
How will we dance when our bonds are released,
when only light and air and song remain:
the wind our notes, the flowing streams our chords,
when grace makes every melody complete?

Ripples

Brother, I live another life these days.
I walk through level forests where strange wings
convene in brambles for the journey south.
Our river changes course with every storm,
and changing marshes at the river's mouth,
abundant, swarm with life. Here each voice sings,
melodious and joyful, in midair

and each sweet echo vibrates everywhere.
The resonance of earth repeats their sound
until creation sings in harmony.
And images on tidal swells transform
reflections, until mirrored ecstasy
fills every breath of air. Ripples surround
each stone along the shore, cascading through

each other, and, transfiguring, renew
the water's surface and the flooded land.
I celebrate each echo. I rejoice
in every change as these reflections form
new images, now mirrored in my voice
in language we, together, understand:
a quiet whispering of joyful praise.

The Visit

Sister, we came to see you in this place
after so many years. The open road
narrowed and turned to half-lanes as we neared
the monastery where you'd come to pray.
And as we turned uphill, the forest cleared:
we saw the church ahead. A small stream flowed
across a culvert, watering the land.

We only had an hour. I had planned
to speak my life in phrases tinged with loss
but joy made me forget. And so I spoke
of blissful episodes, the interplay
of light and wind and water, to invoke
a sense of beauty, there, beneath the cross
hanging behind you in that quiet room.

But even those clipped words seemed to consume
our moments, and the hour's quiet bell
signalled an end, and waving, you withdrew.
We went into the church, watched the array
of candles burning for us all, and knew
a lasting peace as we heard voices swell
behind a screen, singing a song of grace.

Index

Poem titles are in bold and the first lines are in regular text with page numbers on the right.

Along this rockface every cautious tread	*26*
A man lay dying in a shuttered room	*35*
A man stood at a crucible. It glowed	*13*
A man, languid within his cell, once heard	*38*
Another Kind of Beauty	**49**
Aqua de Vida	**48**
At Chartres	**78**
At dawn the forest's garlands, wreathed in haze,	*48*
A tree, growing nearby, thrust down its roots	*25*
Ave Maria	**40**
Be the Mirror of Life in the Eyes of the Dove	**60**
Bird Song	**17**
Bridge	**9**
Bridge Across the River	**39**
Brother, although I'm blind, yet I can see	*90*
Brother, I am the incense and the smoke,	*86*
Brother, I found some shelter in a cave	*82*
Brother, I live another life these days.	*94*
Brother, I stand in shadows gently cast	*80*
Brother, I went to Chartres and wept for you,	*78*
Brother, low branches hung above streambanks.	*84*
Brother, the path grew hard. In my descent	*88*
Brother, the skiing slopes look almost groomed	*72*
Brother, the work consumes. I read. I write.	*74*
Brother, we walked in silence to the place	*92*
Brother, you did not come to see me leave.	*70*
Calibrations	**69**
Candleflame	**22**
Candlemaker	**10**

Cantata	24
Canticle	41
Charismata	59
Cien Ovejas	44
Claritatis	56
Climbing	8
Coloratura	58
Consolation	77
Correspondence	67
Dark Night	**88**
Dear Brother, I acquired everything	*68*
Dear Sister, I've found paradise. It dwells	*73*
Earthquakes	14
Emptiness	21
Epithalamium	53
Eudaimonia	25
Expect no voices. Do not look for words	*61*
Fall, The	19
Fallen branches define our wilderness,	*39*
Feather	62
Fisherman	84
Fountain	51
From Isola 2000	72
From La Brigue	71
From the Baie des Anges	76
From the Edge	89
From Three Islands	87
Garden of Nuts, The	7
Gentleness	27
Glassmaker	13
Goldsmith	15
Goodness	28
Great Silence	74

Her voice gives energy, her voice invites	*59*
Her voice weaves light, her measures interlace	*63*
"I can't explain. I felt dark wings surround	*20*
I fell among the briars, brambles, spines.	*6*
I followed her. We found ourselves in light	*8*
I walk our river's forest every day	*36*
I wanted us to pause when light declined	*19*
I've seen no doves or tongues of flame. I've seen	*41*
Inner Light of Blossoms, The	**54**
In the Garden	**3**
Interior Melodies	**85**
Intertwined Light	**86**
Intricate Forms Lead to Contemplation	**36**
Is How a Person Becomes a Flowering Orchard, The	**42**
It's hard to see in daylight, since the sun	*54*
Kindness	**30**
Last Journey	**90**
Lavender Blossoms	**81**
Leaves falling in the forest: who will mourn	*47*
Light moves as unformed image, and the glass	*56*
Loom	**16**
Lorica of St. Patrick	**52**
Mariposa	**45**
Marriage	**23**
Muérome de Amores, Carillo	**38**
Music Vigil	**35**
My Brother Sun, my dearest Sister Moon,	*67*
My eyesight must be failing. I can see	*41*
My own experience is different: I	*21*
Note from Paradise	**73**
On wooden frames, the thread,	*16*
One Breath, The	**50**

One Song	75
Our last ascent: the summit within sight.	30
Our way was blocked by heaps of fallen stone.	14
Out of the earth itself, out of the stones,	42
Palisades	5
Panis Angelicus	47
Patience	29
Peace	31
Petals	18
Pilgrimage	4
Recessional	70
Reflection	63
Relinquishing, The	68
Requested by the young bride, she arrives	53
Rhapsody	57
Ripples	94
Robe of Beauty	43
rose with thirteen petals greets the air, A	3
Rustic Cross	92
Self-control	26
Shared Path, The	80
She lives within her song, but does not live	37
She's dressed in layers of reserved brocade,	23
She's singing as we walk. There is no voice	24
Shekhinah	46
Shoemaker	11
Silence in candlelight. Red incense burns	50
single dove flew in the opened door, A	62
Sister, a mountain pool called to me.	83
Sister, I found a house in St. Pancrace.	75
Sister, I found a mountain lake, whose banks	87
Sister, I summon words. I speak the names	79
Sister, in Seaside Alps, the paved road ends	71
Sister, my father owned an aging car	69
Sister, night-walking above timberline	85

Sister, simplicity my only gift,	81
Sister, some nights are filled with nameless things–	77
Sister, the light no longer found my eyes.	89
Sister, the tiny flowers at my feet,	93
Sister, these bones are numbered. All this pain	91
Sister, we came to see you in this place	95
Smoke curled from a chimnied tile roof:	15
Some say we should abandon everything:	55
The air is veiled when she sings, lamp light	46
The boundaries of experience dissolve	49
The colors of her strong voice interweave,	40
The jewelled wings in motion intersect	45
The last terrace was smaller than the rest:	31
The next ring held a vineyard, well-designed,	27
The next shop housed a shoemaker, whose task	12
The workshop crafted candles, elements	10
They chanted lyrics as they walked along	52
This woodland path I follow twists and turns	57
Thorns	**6**
Tongue of Fire, A	**79**
Twisted Knot, The	**91**
Ubi Caritas	**37**
Untier of Knots	**93**
Untier of Knots, The	**12**
Via Pulchritudinis	**55**
Viriditas	**61**
Visit, The	**95**
Walking along the path, we looked for ways	17
Water of Life	**82**
We came across a woman sitting outside	11
We came across a woman sitting outside	76
We came upon a man building a frame,	28
We could not bear the light directly, so	58
We find the mountain's base, and find a wall	5

We found a field newly harvested,	*29*
We found a small plant growing in the rift	*18*
We found an empty house, completely dark,	*22*
We had not asked for water or for shade	*7*
We rested in the orchard for a time,	*8*
We walk the riverwood and celebrate	*60*
We work our gardens as we can, provide	*51*
We wrap ourselves within her robe of song,	*43*
"Where can we go?" I asked, looking around	*4*
Whirlpool	**83**
Wings	**20**

Publication Credits

Grateful acknowledgement is made to the editors of the following publications in which poems from *The Terraced Mountain* first appeared:

Angle Poetry: "Shekhinah"

Bridgewater International Poetry Festival Anthology: "The One Breath"

Free State Review: "Charismata"

Frederick Literary Review: "Petals"

Levure Litteraire: "Be the Mirror of Life in the Eyes of the Dove"

Life and Legends: "Intertwined Light," "Ripples," "Untier of Knots"

Modern Poetry Quarterly Review: "Music Vigil"

riverbabble: "This Is How a Person Becomes a Flowering Orchard"

San Diego Poetry Annual: "Coloratura"

Vending Machine: Poetry for Change: "Candleflame"

Verse Virtual: "Canticle," "Feather"

About the Author

W.F. Lantry

W.F. Lantry, native of San Diego, is a widely published prize winning poet who has been featured in literary journals and readings nationally and internationally. He currently lives in the Washington, DC area.

His poetry collections are *The Structure of Desire* (Little Red Tree 2012), winner of a 2013 Nautilus Award in Poetry, and a chapbook, *The Language of Birds* (Finishing Line Press 2011), a lyric retelling of Attar's Conference of the Birds. A new collection *The Book of Maps* is forthcoming. Other publication credits encompass print and online journals and anthologies in more than twenty countries on five continents, with his work translated into French, Arabic, Italian and Uzbek. He was the founding featured author of *Eclectica*, and new work has appearedin numerous publications in many countries including: Canada, Mexico, Scotland, France, Germany, Austria, Czech Republic, Syria, Bosnia & Herzegovina, Turkey, Israel, Indonesia, India, China and the UK.

He has given readings of his work in California, Connecticut, Massachusetts, New York, Tennessee, Texas, Maryland, Pennsylvania, Virginia and Washington, DC. While in Nice, he participated in *Interspace*, a project seeking to unify Poetry, Philosophy, Music and Visual Art. As part of the *Interspace* project, he gave readings at the *Musée Chéret* and *Galerie Ponchettes* in Nice, Centre Pompidou in Paris, *La Sapienza, Università di Roma* in Italy and collaborated on a multi media event presented at the *Roccabella* in Monte Carlo under the patronage of Prince Albert. Recently he was featured at the Bowery Poetry Club Carmine Street Metrics Series and *Fictionaut* Reading at KGB in New York City; Whispered Words Anthology Reading in Ontario; the Bridgewater International Poetry Festival in Virginia; Bethesda Literary Festival Award Ceremony, Kensington Row Poetry Series and Kensington International Day of the Book Celebration in Maryland; and the *Cha: An Asian Literary Journal* AWP Reading at Harvard. He launched his first full length collection with a reading and reception at Poets House in New York City.

Recent honors include: a Nautilus Book Award in Poetry; the *Potomac Review* Poetry Prize, *Old Red Kimono* LaNelle Daniel Prize, *The Linnet's Wing* Audio Poetry Prize (Ireland) and the *Inspired by Tagore* Publication Prize (India); the *Crucible* Editors' Poetry Prize, *Atlanta* Review International Publication Prize, the *CutBank* Patricia Goedicke Prize in Poetry, *Comment Magazine* Poetry Award (Canada), Lindberg Foundation International Poetry for Peace Prize (Israel), and the National Hackney Literary Award in Poetry. He has been named finalist four times in the *Premio Mundial Fernando Rielo de Poesía Mística* (Spain).

Lantry worked with Carolyn Forché in California, where he founded and edited *Eye Prayers*, a small press journal of poetry. He taught for eight years at *L'Université de Nice* in France earning his *License* and *Maîtrise* in Literature, Linguistics and Translation. Boston University awarded him a Fellowship to study with Derek Walcott and George Starbuck, who together directed his thesis; he received an M.A. in English and Creative Writing. He holds a PhD in Literature and Creative Writing from the University of Houston where he worked with Donald Barthelme, Ed Hirsch, Mary Robison and Adam Zagajewski. He was the first in the program to complete a double dissertation, one in Fiction, one in Poetry. He has taught at 12 different Universities on two continents in a variety of fields, most often Literature and Rhetoric, but also in History, World Civilizations and Information Technology. He held the position of Director of Academic Technology at a research university in Washington, DC for 15 years. He served as contributing editor of *Umbrella Journal*, and currently is an associate fiction editor at *JMWW*, and is a founding member of the DC-Area Literary Translators network.

The Terraced Mountain is his second full-length collection.